THE FREEDOM REVOLUTION
AND THE CHURCHES

THE FREEDOM

AND THE

REVOLUTION
CHURCHES

by Robert W. Spike

ASSOCIATION PRESS
NEW YORK

Publisher's stock number: 1551
Library of Congress catalog card number: 64-20240

Printed in the United States of America

To my colleagues
on the staff of the
Commission on Religion and Race
of the National Council of Churches

Preface

What business does a white middle-class church bu-
reaucrat have writing about the freedom movement
in the United States?

One of the most obvious things about the surge of
Negro protest efforts in this country is how little white
people, even supposedly enlightened white people,
have understood the real dynamics of these events.
Church people bear a particular burden of guilt because they have so frequently sounded as if they did
understand the issues, but really did not. They pay
allegiance to a gospel that proclaims the infinite worth
of each human soul in the eyes of God. The major
opinion of church bodies in this country has been that
segregation and discrimination against people on the
basis of color are a sinful denial of that gospel. Brave
souls have from time to time given personal witness
on the streets and in jail in support of that belief. And
yet, until very recently, the churches have been so
caught up in the inertia of a white privileged class
that they have betrayed their gospel and their few
courageous adherents by tokenism and inaction. So

what business does a white johnny-come-lately have in writing about events that he has only recently come to see are going to transform the whole of American society?

Perhaps the only justification for writing this book at all emerges from the very marginal nature of the author's involvement. Three advantages may be wrung from being a white man-come-late to the heart of the struggle.

First, he sees with freshness what the Negro leadership and followership have really accomplished in these past years—facts sometimes blurry to those who have been long at it and caught up in it all their lives.

Second, he may serve as an interpreter to those other white churchmen who feel something of the stirring of the movement, but who are still impeded by their fears and ignorance of what it is all about.

And third, moving from one segment of the nation's life to another, terribly aware of the widening cracks in our old social myths, he may convey something of the urgency of the times.

This last point, this urgency, is where I hope most to be useful; for the urgency is not related simply to the possibility that the nation may suffer more tragic internal strife. That is certainly an important concern. But beyond that, in a world caught between riches and the threat of death, this revolution for human rights in the nation where both have their firmest anchor, has significance for the whole human family.

And that is the true nature of its theological significance. God's fate is never at stake. Men who call on

God always do so at their own peril. They must judge their living by that calling. Their sins rise up to haunt them, and also to goad them to a new order of living. Let mercy roll down as water, and justice as a mighty stream.

These times are eschatological. Between riches and death, the Negro people of this nation have begun a social revolution that will alter the life of every single person in this nation and in the world, before it is done.

This book, then, is a tract about the events of the immediate past and present in the freedom movement.

To God be the thanks and the praise!

ROBERT W. SPIKE

Contents

9

1. The Decade 1954-1964

The movement toward full equality on the part of the Negro people certainly did not begin when the Supreme Court handed down its historic decision which struck down legal school segregation. The decision was, however, a powerful landmark in the long struggle, and it will remain a watershed event when the history of these times is written.

Only recently has the American public come to know many aspects of the history of Negro resistance in the 300-year span of their existence on this continent.

The myth of a contented and servile slave population is exploded by any study of how slaves were captured and brought here, and of the local rebellions that took place.

Earlier Efforts Toward Freedom

The ante bellum efforts toward freedom are worthy of our study if we really want a picture of how long the struggle has been going on. The efforts of the abolitionists, both in the North and underground among the Negro population in the South, bore real fruit finally in the Emancipation Proclamation, but perhaps even more in the seeds planted in the Negro community—seeds that have come to a new fruition in this century.

The establishment of schools for Negroes on a very large scale after the Civil War in all parts of the North was the final fruit of the Abolitionist Movement. The American Missionary Association founded over 600 schools in the South between the end of the Civil War and the beginning of the twentieth century. These schools were of all levels of competence. Most of them were eventually turned over to the states and became ironically the backbone of the segregated school system. Some of them survive to this day as Negro colleges in the South.

This whole period of "education toward freedom" is now viewed with mixed emotions by Negro Americans. On the one hand, it provided thousands of them with intellectual weapons which passed down from generation to generation, finding their full use in today's struggle.

On the other hand, men like Booker T. Washington seem, in retrospect, to have been too subservient, too trusting that once educational standards were achieved, there would be a wholesale opening of the white society. To this day, there are still those white people who proclaim the need for a few more decades of "education" until full opportunity should be granted Negroes.

the overarching institutions of our society might be mobilized to bring really decisive changes in the society.

This was by way of being more of a subconscious feeling than a part of a deliberate plan, however, and is more obvious in retrospect than it was at the time.

Protest Demonstrations

The next decisive event was the Montgomery, Alabama, bus boycott in December, 1955. Rosa Parks decided that she simply had had enough and refused to move to the back of the bus, thereby triggering the events that led to the boycott. A whole new indigenous movement was set in motion. The young minister of the Dexter Avenue Baptist Church, Martin Luther King, recently returned from seminary and graduate work in the North, was drawn into the leadership of this movement quite beyond his own expectation and planning. With Ralph Abernathy, another minister in Montgomery, Martin King became the leader of the Montgomery Improvement Association, which organized Negro citizens into an effective boycott of the buses. It was as if the breaking point of suffering, humiliation, and quiet desperation had come. The white community reacted with stunned shock when it became apparent how widespread was the determination of the Negro community. There followed bombings, legal harassments, and the spreading of boycotts to other cities.

It can only now be seen as providential that there

was on the scene at this moment a man whose Christian understanding and knowledge of Gandhian nonviolent tactics could be brought into the leadership of this new determination. Certainly Martin King did not expect to start a movement that would spread across the South when he took up his responsibility. He saw it as his responsibility, as a local pastor, to guide and shape the Montgomery Improvement Association. However, people in other parts of the South began to be encouraged by the *élan* of the King-led movement. It is an ironic but not well-known fact that the boycott did not finally integrate the Montgomery buses. A court order was necessary to do that.

The next important set of events centers around a technique of protest called "the sit-ins," encouraged by Dr. King's example. Students in Greensboro, North Carolina, began sitting at the segregated lunch counters in five-and-dime stores. This student involvement, beginning in 1958 and 1959, spread to other cities. The Congress of Racial Equality, an organization which had been active in protest movements for two decades, helped in the original preparation of students. Nashville became the next center of effective student sit-ins and indeed has produced an unusually high percentage of the students who helped to form the Student Nonviolent Co-ordinating Committee.

The freedom rides began on May 4, 1961, on a projected test trip of segregated facilities involved in interstate commerce. This trip was from Washington, D.C., to New Orleans. It was accompanied by intense persecution and violence in many of the cities where the group attempted to be served in white sides of the bus terminal restaurants. There were many subsequent freedom rides in which integrated groups tried to make their witness. These were the first methods used by northern white ministers in any sizable way to express their own deep conviction about segregation. Rock Hill, South Carolina; Anniston, Alabama; Birmingham, Alabama; Tallahassee, Florida; Jackson, Mississippi—all have been scenes of intense harassment visited on integrated groups. Finally, the Interstate Commerce Commission, in a historic ruling, effected the complete desegregation of bus, train, and air terminal facilities.

An accompanying move tested tourist facilities along highways in border states, primarily Route 40, the main road between Washington, D.C., and New York City in those days. Many of the restaurants along this road discriminated until the pressure became intense.

The summer of 1962 was in the nation's news because of racial struggle in Albany, Georgia, a town where the Negro population suffered rigid segregation and violence. Many forces joined to try to wring some concessions in employment and opened public accommodations. Martin King was imprisoned for a long time in Albany during this protest. Many northern clergymen participated. Albany, however, resulted in a kind of deadlock of accomplishments.

The spring of 1963, nine years after the historic Supreme Court decision, saw the real breakthrough. This does not mean that there had not been many other accomplishments in school desegregation. Little Rock, New Orleans, and Clinton, Tennessee, had all seen major accomplishment because of the bravery of small children and their parents. However, in 1963, Birmingham, where a strong Negro protest movement under Fred Shuttlesworth had existed for some time, was one of the most intensely segregated cities in the South. Long months of negotiation had resulted in no breakthrough so far as Negro employment or public accommodations were concerned. In the spring of that year, the long frustration of the Negro population brought them into the streets in strong protest. Again, Martin Luther King went to jail for leading demonstrations. Hundreds of people, including large numbers of young persons, daily faced high-pressure fire hoses, police dogs, and inescapable jailing for what they believed to be their rights. "The Letter from Birmingham Jail" by Martin Luther King will go down as one of the classic statements of what was felt at that time. Other cities erupted into ugly discord. Cambridge, Maryland, and Danville, Virginia, are particularly remembered, for there, the violent use of force to suppress peaceful demonstrations was most evident. And, in Jackson, Mississippi, Medgar Evers, the state leader of the NAACP, was shot in the back at night as he entered his home.

Commission on Religion and Race

In the midst of the tuning up of this violent conflict between the races, many white Americans for the first time faced realistically the results of hundreds of years of the suppression of Negro Americans. President Kennedy, who had himself recently come through the experience of having to integrate the University of Mississippi with federal force, moved to prepare a comprehensive Civil Rights Bill designed to bring redress for some of the most historic grievances and some of the most glaring examples of civil wrongs. In that same period, the National Council of Churches established the Commission on Religion and Race to move directly into the heart of the struggle and to bring the resources of the churches into a ministry leading to the quickest achievement of justice for a healing reconciliation.

The March on Washington in the summer of 1963 brought into peaceful focus all the deep feelings of Negro and concerned white people. This great demonstration of conviction, perhaps more than any other event, became a symbol of commitment to make drastic changes in our customary way of life that would bring about some of the opportunities that Negroes had so long been denied.

Violence, however, had only a moment's respite, for the fall brought more tragedy. The most horrifying was the bombing of the Tenth Street Baptist Church in Birmingham, Alabama, where four little Sunday school girls were killed.

And then the murder of the President in Dallas.

The Civil Rights Bill

The concerted efforts of the coalition of civil rights forces that had been created to support the March on Washington held together through the winter months of 1963 and 1964, urging the passage of the Civil Rights Bill. Finally, the bill was passed by Congress in June, 1964. The persistent efforts of the religious forces of the country were credited with having made the difference between the passage of this strong bill and the failures of other years. In anticipation of the passage of the bill, many southern communities began to work toward peaceful means of accepting it, particularly in the area of opening public accommodations. Thus, when the bill was finally passed, a great many places immediately complied with it.

The summer of 1964, the tenth year of the fateful decade, was noted primarily for the concentration of a massive effort to change the traditional ways of doing things in Mississippi. The effort was known as the Mississippi Summer Project. Hundreds of students recruited by the Council of Federated Organizations (COFO, the Mississippi united organization of NAACP, CORE, SCLC, SNCC) were trained for their tasks by the National Council of Churches and then sent into the field to do remedial teaching and community organization for citizenship among the impoverished Negroes of Mississippi. The program was not designed to be a confrontation directly challenging white segregated facilities and customs. Rather, it was intended to begin a more basic job of bringing morale,

training, and experience to a large number of younger
Mississippi Negroes so that they might be equipped
to participate in the drastic changes coming over the
region. Despite the peaceful intention of the program,
it was met by many hostile and distorted accounts of
its purpose. Before the bulk of the students arrived
on the scene, two persons who were to lead the program and one student were killed near Philadelphia,
Mississippi. Their deaths alerted national attention
and brought about a stronger measure of federal pressure on the state government and also the presence of
larger numbers of FBI agents. Consequently, despite
recurring harassment, there were no other serious in-
cidents.

The summer of 1964 also saw the outbreak of rioting in Harlem, New York City; Rochester, New York;
Chicago; and various New Jersey satellite cities. This
kind of rioting had long been predicted if drastic
changes did not come. In the main, the riots were
caused by the pent-up frustration of unemployed
young Negroes reacting to some incident of discrimination or alleged police brutality. Lawless activity like
looting and violence resulted. This provided many
people in the white community with an easy rationali-
zation for declaring that the Negro revolution was going too far and for expressing their fears of what was
happening.

At the end of the decade, one could see how mo-
mentous a pattern was woven by all these strikingly
different kinds of protest, tragedy, and response. The
year 1964 did not find the Negro free of the results of

discrimination. The problems of discrimination in housing, of inequality in education, and of increasing unemployment caused as much by automation as anything else, meant that unrest and suspicion were very real. Nonetheless, there had been a shaking loose in American complacency that was significant. There had been great gains made, symbolized best perhaps by the Supreme Court Decision of 1954 and the Civil Rights Act of 1964. Most important of all, there was a generation of determined Negroes who never again could be pushed around or discounted.

2. The Varieties of Protest

To the uninvolved the civil rights struggle in recent years has seemed like a confusing outpouring of alphabet soup—NAACP, CORE, SCLC, SNCC, NSM, and many other local groups.

Though it is not true that the organized civil rights groups have *created* the tension situations or even that these groups have in their membership a large percentage of the Negro population of this country, an understanding of their positions helps to open up the nature of the struggle.

Most Negroes are like most white people: they do not want to get involved in any controversial organization. Nevertheless, the desperation that has gripped the Negro who has tried to get an equal place in this society and has been frustrated and blocked, has found its most fruitful outlet in organized groups.

Protest Movements, Black and White

The oldest group still active in the United States is the National Association for the Advancement of Colored People. W. E. B. DuBois was its first distinguished executive. In later days Walter White and now Roy Wilkins have headed the organization.

The organization has been precisely what its name indicates—a membership group made up of both Negro and white persons who have sought by every legal means and by education and information to advance the cause of the colored man in this country. The organization works through local and regional chapters. The program varies from place to place, but the national organization exercises strong leadership.

Most of the organized gains made by Negroes in this country during the past decades in the field of desegregation of schools and public facilities, and in getting remedial legislation, have had NAACP vigorous participation. They maintain an excellent legislative office in Washington, under the able direction of Clarence Mitchell. The historic legal battles for desegregation have been conducted largely under what is called the "Inc." fund—that is, the NAACP Legal Defense Fund, Inc.—a separate corporation working closely with the central body. Thurgood Marshall was its distinguished director for many years. That position is now held by Jack Greenberg.

The NAACP has not been noted for its direct action—such as picketing and demonstrating—until very recently, when it has joined in some of these activities. Because of its age and tradition, NAACP has been under heavy attack from younger, more aggressive Negro organizations. It has managed to find a liaison relationship with the established liberal forces in this country, nationally with the Democratic Party and the major labor groups.

The NAACP has often opposed the rasher action of student and direct action groups. It has become very sensitive to criticism that it is conservative, pointing justifiably to the record of solid accomplishment over the years. Roy Wilkins and other leaders value highly their reputation for responsibility. They believe they have a role in forming the national liberal consensus and do not want to jeopardize it. Mr. Wilkins is a brilliant, articulate man who can phrase with equal sharpness the Negro's just grievance and his brethren's seeming rashness in the struggle.

There are NAACP chapters which are more militant than the national position and many less so, although there is a continuing pressure to move the NAACP into more aggressive action. Medgar Evers, the martyred Mississippi state director of NAACP, has become the symbol for much of that kind of action.

Many chapters are led by Negro professional men, doctors, lawyers, dentists, whose natural style of life is not geared to precipitous action. Critics of the NAACP accuse it of being too dominated by these middle-class Negroes and by the white liberals who have shared in its Board of Directors from the beginning.

The Urban League, founded at the time of World War I, has consistently fixed its attention on developing economic opportunities for people of all races. It has done this by developing support from a broad interracial coalition of influential community and business leaders. In many communities it has even become a Red Feather agency and enjoys great respectability. In the forties and fifties many people believed the organization to be almost moribund. Now under the energetic direction of Whitney Young, the League has achieved a new burst of life. It is increasingly recognized that one of the major areas of trouble is unemployment and lack of job opportunity. The League has achieved a new importance in developing such opportunities. The League is a logical place of entrance into effective participation in the freedom revolution for many whites who can really do something in their businesses and communities. Because the League has held very closely to its focus of economic opportunity, it has not become the butt of so much attack from the militants. As a matter of fact, many have been surprised by the kind of coalition participation into which the League has entered, for example as a co-sponsor of the March on Washington. Young, along with Wilkins, is frequently consulted in Washington on racial matters.

The first major direct action organization in the pattern we know today was the Congress of Racial Equality. CORE began during World War II to break patterns of discrimination in places of public accommodation. This was, in the beginning, largely in the North; but, in the years directly after the war, Bayard Rustin led the first interracial testing team into the border states and the South. CORE's approach has always been firmly wedded to nonviolence although in recent years this has been severely tested by the aggressive commitment of some of its chapters.

CORE was a very small loosely organized organization until the late fifties when it effectively organized the original sit-ins in North and South Carolina. CORE has had a phenomenal growth of chapters all over the country, although its major strength is still in northern cities. In fact CORE is still a loosely federated organization of local chapters; however, the national organization under James Farmer has increasingly tried to bring cohesion and disciplined national action to the organization. In Mississippi and Louisiana there are activities under CORE auspices, but the northern cities chapters have been the most active. In most places CORE has attracted the more deeply alienated and hostile Negro, impatient with the mode of the NAACP and eager for action. They have led sit-ins and demonstrations of all sorts. There have been times of great internal tension when the established leadership has tried to contain wildcat chapter activities which seemed intent on direct action for its own sake, rather than on evaluation of strategies in relation to goal. Gradually those who favor a broader spectrum of activity, including concentration on political activity, have won a larger say in the organization. James Farmer occupies a unique role in the leadership spectrum of the movement. He has often been able to stay in touch with the more angry and hostile groups of Negro activists and at the same time to communicate with the anxious established community which is looking more eagerly for peace than it is for justice. He often seems something of a mysterious figure, not quite trusted by many people. Much of this has to do with the boundary line role he has to play. Mickey Schwerner, one of the three young workers murdered in Mississippi in the summer of 1964, was a CORE worker. It was his program—community-center-oriented political action—representing the new thrust of CORE concern, that prompted the Ku Klux Klan to finger him and his companions for extinction.

The Southern Christian Leadership Conference draws its central inspiration from Martin Luther King. This is both its strength and its weakness. It is an even more loosely federated organization than CORE, being an association of local movements largely in southern cities where Dr. King and his associates have preached and led demonstrations. SCLC has added the distinctive flavor and fervor to the movement that raised it from a bitter struggle for Negro justice to a religious struggle for morality in the nation. The awarding of the Nobel Prize to Dr. King was a fitting recognition that he did in fact become "the conscience of the nation" as he was called in the March on Washington. Here is a man who has been thrust by events into a world arena as a symbol of Christian witness in the face of hostility. The world has responded to him in a way that few Christian preachers have experienced. His courage and his restraint put the kind of stamp of righteousness on the movement that made it possible for the whole nation to take a new look at itself in the spring of 1963.

This awesome role of being a world symbol has not been assumed without cost. It has meant that SCLC as an organization has not matured into effective long-term programing, with the major exception of its

Voter Registration and Citizenship Education Project. This program under the initial direction of Andrew Young, now the Executive Director of SCLC, and with the co-operation of the Field Foundation and the United Church Board for Homeland Ministries, has done solid work in training people of the rural South in how to get people to register to vote.

Dr. King and SCLC are also often under attack by SNCC and others because of the widespread popularity they enjoy with white liberal groups. They believe him to be too accommodating to white opinion and, like Roy Wilkins and Whitney Young, too often invited to the White House.

The Student Nonviolent Co-ordinating Committee sprang from the bosom of CORE and was nurtured in early days by close association with SCLC. SNCC is much more a state of mind than an organization, although it has accomplished a formidable list of objectives in its brief history. Its origins in the sit-in movement are never far from its activity although the scope of its work has been greatly broadened. SNCC is characterized by the all-out commitment of its members to drastic changes in the society which overtly and subtly have kept Negroes in bondage. There are many white participants, but the group is controlled by strongly self-conscious Negroes, who view with increasing suspicion anyone who has any ties to the "power structure," local or national. They remain a movement more than an organization by intense and passionate devotion to direct action under hostile conditions, living on the barest subsistence, and rarely trusting anyone outside that brotherhood of danger.

Jim Foreman is the executive director; but, in fact, leadership has been shared by many others, preeminently John Lewis and Bob Moses, the originator of the Mississippi Summer Project.

It is not accidental that Mississippi became the center of the activities of SNCC in 1963 and 1964. Mississippi as the center of the most outrageous persecution of Negroes was the citadel that most needed attacking. In its heavy concentration on Mississippi, the extreme egalitarian ideology of SNCC became intensified. The Mississippi Freedom Democratic Party was an outgrowth of it. Its weakness, however, resides in a romanticizing of "the people" so that all effective organization is suspect; and, in addition, the movement becomes vulnerable to any outside influence which, using the language of equality, can exercise leadership. Nonetheless, SNCC was the catalyst that started the major changes which are coming about in Mississippi and some other places. They attract the idealism of the student generation, and the whole nation owes them a debt, not only for their brave accomplishments, but for the example of virile Negro action which they have presented.

While SNCC is being described, it is well to mention again COFO—the Council of Federated Organizations. This is the Mississippi federation of local units of SCLC, CORE, NAACP, and SNCC under which the unified civil rights push on many fronts was conducted in 1963 and 1964. From the beginning, however, SNCC was the dominant group, by virtue both of workers and of financial support. The other organizations, particularly NAACP, became increasingly annoyed with this domination, and have begun to seek other forms through which to work. If all the organizations had put as much energy as SNCC into this combined effort, the differences might have been avoided, although the extremely divergent ideologies of the groups would probably have made them incompatible anyway.

The Northern Student Movement grew out of the New England Student Christian Movement originally as a volunteer organization for students to engage in tutoring programs in the black ghettos. After two years, the students who had set up many able programs of this sort in a number of northern cities became convinced that they had to expand their activity to more basic community action programs. They have begun to move somewhat in the pattern of SNCC, although with a deeper social analysis, and are attempting to develop programs for "the powerless to obtain power" in the ghetto through organizing rent strikes, community unions, and similar activities. William Strickland is presently their able leader.

SDS (Students for a Democratic Society) is a similar student organization with slightly divergent program plans, working in both Negro and white urban poverty pockets, with a strong interest in basic community change.

ACT is a relatively new committee of people from the major northern cities representing very militant positions on direct action. Lawrence Landry of Chicago, Jesse Gray of New York, and Julius Hobson of

Washington are the names most associated with this organization, if it can be called that.

Black Muslims, Black Nationalists, Freedom Now Party

Other national groups frequently mentioned are the Black Muslims, the Black Nationalists, and the Freedom Now Party. The Muslims, under the leadership of Elijah Muhammed, are over 30 years old as an organized group, but only within recent years have they come into prominence. They preach a kind of black superiority doctrine, which is largely a "you can't trust any white man" theme. Malcolm X was the spokesman who first raised this organization to national attention. He severed his connections with Elijah, made a pilgrimage to visit authentic Muslim centers in Africa (which do not teach doctrines of racial exclusiveness) and returned to the United States to establish a true Muslim center. His brutal murder shocked the whole Negro community. His militancy was admired by millions who did not share his ideology.

The Black Muslim "threat" has been greatly exaggerated in this country. It is often posed as the exact balance of the Ku Klux Klan and other terrorist organizations. Careful study of the Black Muslims indicates that it is a powerfully close-knit brotherhood which gives a new sense of dignity and purpose to its Negro members who have been psychologically crushed by white society. Until the feud with Malcolm they had not engaged in violence or terrorism, generally remaining under a strong discipline. This restraint gives the appearance of being drawn like a tight spring, ready to fly into aggressive action. They have succeeded in frightening quite a few white people who fear the worst from their mysterious black neighbors. Most Negroes who would certainly not share their doctrine are loath to criticize them. They *do* share their analysis, in the main, of the wide-ranging and deeply penetrating nature of the white society's exclusion of the black. If the summer of 1963 had not seen the March on Washington, the beginning of the Civil Rights Bill struggle, and other evidences of national concern over the social crisis, the Muslims and the Black Nationalists might really have made headway among a terribly discouraged and embittered people.

The Black Nationalist and Freedom Now Party people represent an even smaller group of actual members. They share the mystique of black superiority with the Muslims but without the religious structure or the unrealistic solution of partitioning the country. In fact, they do not have long-range goals, only the mobilization of immediate action under totally Negro auspices to protest injustices and to dramatize them.

Church Bodies for Direct Action

It would not now be a comprehensive picture in describing the various organized forces at work, moving toward charges in race relations, if the churches were omitted here.

From 1963 onward, church people (and synagogues

as well) have begun to form organizations and to shape existing bodies for direct action. This represents a decided change in position. Not since the abolitionist period have the churches and their people become as conscious of their guilt and their need for action as in recent months. Formerly church people were urged to work through existing organizations, but in the spring of 1963 it became apparent that the church bodies themselves needed to use their powerful resources directly in the struggle. The interreligious Chicago Conference on Religion and Race in January of that year set a mood for concerted action with its four faith groups that has had many concrete expressions since that time.

The establishment of the National Council of Churches Commission on Religion and Race in June of 1964 marked an historic turning point in the life of Protestantism and Orthodoxy. For the first time a direct action ecumenical agency was commissioned by the top representatives of the denominations to give leadership in the public sphere in the area of racial conflict. Several of the larger denominations established special bodies or processes (the United Presbyterian Commission was actually authorized before the National Council Commission) to aid in a common program.

In many cities, Commissions on Religion and Race have been established, sometimes interreligiously and sometimes only on a Protestant ecumenical basis. The natures of these commissions differ. Some are consulting co-ordinating bodies. Others form programs of action and reconciliation.

Effectiveness of Protest Organizations

As the whole field of the civil rights organizational paraphernalia is surveyed, two questions seem appropriate: How trustworthy are these organizations, and How effective are they?

The question "How trustworthy are they?" is raised, because of the blanket condemnation made equally of all bodies involved in civil rights: namely, that they are all Communist or Communist sympathizers. This accusation in some quarters covers everything from the National Council of Churches to ACT and beyond.

Without being a J. Edgar Hoover, it is of course impossible to know the details of who is or who isn't secretly a Communist agent. All obvious tests, however, would indicate that there is no influential Communist tinge in the movement in its broadest stream. The NAACP is, of course, very conscious of this threat, having moved through a time in the thirties and forties when Communists did try to infiltrate the organization as they did organized labor. A very few people who have participated in some of the student movements and in the more extreme nationalist movements have identifiable records of association with Communist front organizations. There are a few who have distinct sympathies with the Cuban revolution and the Chinese revolution. These people have been easily identified and in the main are discounted. Their influence is not felt in policy making or strategy. There are those who confuse with a "Communist" influence the deep bitterness that many of the more militant Negroes feel toward the limited federal action in the South. John Lewis' reply to that charge is perhaps the most telling: "Negroes do not need the Communists to tell us that something is wrong in Mississippi." There are undoubtedly some groups who would like to manipulate themselves into positions of influence in the movement for reasons of opposition to the government. The only way this can happen is for a vacuum to be left by those who are for civil rights out of deep loyalty to and love for this country. If people are afraid of "guilt by association" or possible unknowing association with undesirable people, then they leave the field to whoever is less squeamish. It is possible that a deeply alienated radical movement can develop out of this civil rights struggle which will stand permanently at odds with the main consensus of public opinion. In some forms, that might be a healthy thing for this country, but surely not one built on simple justice which the majority bars from its concern.

Another aspect to the "trustworthiness" question is the stability of these organizations. To the extent that these groups are really engaged in the struggle in daily events, they are not run like structured bureaucracies within the establishment. They work on the run. Events modify and change their plans. People are working under extreme pressure and often fatigue. And they remain people with all the frailties of human nature. Therefore, letters may remain unanswered, plans seem infuriatingly vague and inconclusive. Individuals hate other individuals even though the cause they serve is a high one in the name of justice and love. A revolution is not neat, and it is amazing how carefully some things are co-ordinated in the light of the tension and the pressure.

How effective are these organizations? It would be disheartening, perhaps, to take a poll of how many Negroes, and concerned whites, actually belong to these civil rights groups. They represent a very small percentage indeed. In fact, the real source of much trouble is the fact that many of the most disadvantaged Negroes do not have any trust that organizations, national or local, can do anything to help them. They are either cynical or apathetic about them. Those who participated in the riots of the summer of 1964 in New York, Rochester, Paterson, Philadelphia were not members of groups. They were the young, unemployed, embittered black men who saw no hope for themselves or their families in a rich society moving by them, oblivious to them. More and more groups are trying to organize these people and others like them. Who are the leaders of the leaderless? Who speaks for "me"? These are questions more and more being asked by Negroes who want deep, basic changes in the society, to give them a chance in their lifetime.

Many of the organizations, in the light of this, are turning their attention increasingly to political action, geared in with economic problems, as the key to meeting the needs of the really dispossessed.

3. The Gap Between Black and White

There are times, when you observe a group of students, black and white, sitting around together discussing a common problem with earnestness and frankness, that you believe we are progressing rapidly toward an integrated society.

Then you move away from that experience. You listen to a couple of ladies talking in the front of a bus in a southern city: "See, *they* go to the back of the bus anyway. They really like it that way."

You sit on the edge of a conversation with some couples around a fireplace in a relaxed friendly evening in the suburbs. "I'm against all this killing stuff down South. But I don't want *them* for neighbors. That's *my* right, isn't it?"

More disturbing still is how seldom you get to hear the suspicion and distrust personally expressed by Negroes, if you are white. But you remember the hurt look in the Negro colleague's eyes when you have seemed to cut him out of decision making. There is the blank wall of noncommunication when you blithely discuss race relations in a restaurant with your companions while the Negro waiter is within hearing distance.

And then you think back to that idyllic scene of interracial student enterprise and remember some other things. You recall the confusion when a really liberated white girl slips into "niggrah" under the stress of debate. You remember the insistence that a certain decision is right because it was made by the "blacks" present, and the barely suppressed resentment from the white students.

Attitudes

It would seem that as the long-delayed steps of desegregation in our society are at last being taken, the gap between Negroes and whites in terms of ease of communication and true integration is continuing to widen.

This gap is, of course, difficult to measure or to document in any way. For every instance of tension and hostility, an example of progress can be cited. There is the whole continuum of attitudes still existing in this country, from hateful, white supremacists to the embittered black isolationist. In between are all kinds of opinions and feelings: (a) those whites who are fearful of Negroes because they have had no contact with them or have had unpleasant contacts; (b) those earnest whites who stoutly proclaim their lack of prejudice and then buckle under when it comes time to act on it, as in residential segregation; (c) those whites who devotedly work for racial justice, but with a kind of grimness and a lack of objectivity that make the "white liberal" tag a common epithet among certain Negro groups; (d) those Negroes who have limited contact with whites except as distant figures and who don't want to get involved; (e) those Negroes who have worked closely with whites, have some white friends, but believe the situation is really stacked against them by the white majority; (f) those Negroes who have worked their way to positions of relative security against strong odds, and who dare not risk this security by engaging in civil rights activities; (g) those Negroes who have reached this same level of achievement and who continue to probe and press for the whole Negro people; (h) those Negroes who give free reign to long-suppressed hostility and vent it publicly, either in print, or—in the case of the inarticulate lower class—in rioting.

Assumptions

These are only a few of the kinds of responses that are being made to a new ordering of relations between the races in this country; but in any case there is a probing beneath the surface explanations. This means challenging the classic liberal assumptions that after all there *are* no differences between Negro and white, so you just ignore the supposed difference and things will be all right. This assumption had been held by both black and white, largely educated people, and worked very well within the limitations of an esoteric social group which can exist on the cohesive role of similar ideas and tastes. In such a view, only "education," that is, the raising of all Negroes into this world of refinement and intellectual interests, will finally break down the barriers. The great new fact of the movement of the past few years is that Negroes in great numbers now reject that solution. They have come to see that it is fundamentally patronizing and, in addition, unrealistic. There is actually something more solid to build on in the frank suspicion of unlettered people in the matter of race, than on the self-deception that there are no differences in background and experience with serious consequences for both races.

Perhaps James Baldwin, and those whom he has ignited, have done more than anyone else to impress this upon the consciousness.

The only means whereby we can begin to build a fully integrated society is by facing the real situation of alienation and suspicion that 300 years of history have imposed upon us. This does not mean that we should accept some view of historic determinism. Indeed, it is to be able to free ourselves from that grip that we need to understand how our nation has created a dominant white society and a half-free shadow-black society with such thoroughness that this conception has penetrated very deeply into every corner of the whole nation.

Neither must we wallow in extended psychological probing of what this means in the black or the white psyche. But we do have to understand the far-reaching, almost offhand, gestures that come naturally to someone born white in this country, and the wary, hesitant, always exploratory, reaching-out of someone who is born into the second-class world of Negritude in America.

The burden of *history* and the pressure of everyday *firsthand experience* are what maintain the gap between black and white.

Effects of Slave History

First, we look at the *history* of our country. We are just beginning to understand how deeply the slave history of Negro people has affected our national life. Until very recently history textbooks simply ignored the early black settlers of this country and, reading back from that, wrote off all but white European history as having any significance for civilization as we know it. Segregationists sometimes make the wild claim that the Constitution never was meant to refer to Negroes in the first place, so why talk about Constitutional rights. This was certainly not true of the enlightened founding fathers, but it was undoubtedly true of the majority of people whose state governments ratified the Constitution. Slaves were property first and not persons. A whole region of the country began to build its economy on the slave system after the invention of the cotton gin made cotton growing profitable. Northern white manufacturers profited from this system.

Slavery troubled the conscience of many white Americans long before the Civil War, but only a minority ever escaped from a view of Negroes as primarily subhuman, or at least mentally and socially inferior. This deep disregarding of the personhood of Negroes is the essential white sin in our racial disorder, and it exists today far beyond the blatant segregationist. Though slavery is a hundred years behind us, this history of treating Negroes, either harshly or kindly, as wards of the society is still with our nation.

There are almost no whites, no matter how emancipated, who do not from time to time reflect that patronization. That is one of the reasons why this period is so taxing on personal relationships between black and white.

One often hears white Americans impatiently complain, "See how far we've come in the past few years—school desegregation going on now in every state, a far-reaching Civil Rights Bill that guarantees a wide range of national opportunity regardless of race. Negroes can go anywhere now. Look at the way industry is opening up. What do *they* want?"

Is it any wonder that such expressions are infuriating to Negro Americans? The white majority has finally discovered the humanity of the Negro citizen—something the Negro human being has known about for a long time—and now he is supposed to be grateful for getting his undeniable dues. Whites who expect gratitude for at long last beginning to rectify the sins of our common history constitute part of the problem of the gap between black and white.

What is particularly devastating from the white side of the reaction to this history is how unconscious many are of its existence. They take at face value the ideological affirmations of our society—the Bill of Rights guarantees, and also the assertions of the Declaration of Independence: "We hold these truths to be self-evident, that all men are created equal, that they are endowed by their Creator with certain unalienable Rights, that among these are Life, Liberty, and the pursuit of Happiness." They do not comprehend how chafing it is for these rights to be qualified and limited by the color of one's skin. Some even go so far as to make eloquent affirmations of these basic rights, which are *endowed* by our *Creator,* and then in the second breath explain that these rights must be earned, if one is a Negro.

The more fearful and prejudiced white person often reverses the actual situation in the face of the present challenge to historical two-class citizenship. He loudly proclaims that the civil rights movement is threatening his rights. It is not just, he declares, to take away *his* rights for the sake of redressing Negro grievances. When he is pressed as to what these threatened rights are, they turn out to be special privileges which whites have long enjoyed, by virtue of their majority position, but which do not constitute guaranteed Constitutional rights. There is nothing in the Civil Rights Bill of 1964 or in similar legislation which abrogates or limits any individual rights for the sake of others. What is assured in more specificity is that people may not abuse their freedom of action in order to deprive other people of access to public facilities and the full benefits of governmental support.

This basic confusion about rights and special privileges which history has bestowed on white citizens is a very serious one. It was one of the major causes of the passage of Proposition 14 in the 1964 California elections. This proposition amended the state constitution in such a way as to abrogate existing fair housing laws and seemingly to make it impossible to draft new legislation in this area. It was phrased in language which stressed the buyer's freedom to "sell to whomever" he wished. There never was any question about the ultimate right of the seller to use all the discretion available in final choice of selling property. No legislation compelled an owner to sell to a certain person. All that fair housing legislation prohibited was the denial of the right of a person to advertise publicly his home for sale, to list it as available to the highest bidder, and then to deny that sale on the basis of prejudice because of race or creed. Such an arbitrary denial exceeds the free right of the seller and becomes an intolerable impediment upon the free right of the buyer who responds in all good faith to public advertisement. The collusion of prejudiced property owners becomes an infringement upon the liberties of fellow citizens of other races. It is of course a real question as to whether these are civil rights, or are civil freedoms, long held sacred in our fundamental understanding of what the American system really meant, but always secretly conditioned to mean to apply to white Americans only.

As the national life becomes more and more complicated, the development of a true mass society more and more a reality, the achievement of great mobility is necessary in order to keep the country a going, vital enterprise. This mobility, from one part of the country to the other, from one segment of society to another, can be achieved only by an enlargement of civil rights and civil liberties to include other civil freedoms—inherent in the Declaration of Independence, but never put into practice fully. Thus, this freedom of mobility of residence is not only a part of the unalienable right to life, liberty, and the pursuit of happiness, but it is a social necessity if the nation is to survive with common goals and integrity. As long as whites confuse historic special privileges with rights the gap not only widens, but it takes on the appearance of a festering wound.

Thus far we have looked on the damage from history from the white side. It has an even more deleterious aspect from the black side.

This covert understanding of our national history, as being a creation of the whites only, and only incidentally applicable to blacks, causes tremendous confusion about identity. That is the reason for the upsurge of interest and attention to Negro history in the portfolio of the freedom movement.

In a staff meeting of an interracial agency, a strong argument arose over the relative importance of Negro history in Freedom Schools and other similar enterprises. The staff divided down the middle, the Negro staff members holding out strongly for its very central nature. White staff members objected that it might have some importance; but, after all, the essential thing was to look to the present task and the future accomplishment—where racial background would be extraneous. "I have no interest in my ancestors or yours," one of them asserted. To that came the Negro point of view in reply, "You can be cavalier about history, because you have one."

Negroes have suffered terribly because they have had no viable link with their African heritage. All ties were broken. Even their names are white men's names. And until very recently they were mentioned in historical accounts in the founding and settling of this country as a statistic under property held by certain white pioneer figures. As a matter of fact there were many Negro freedmen who did participate in exploration and settlement. Los Angeles was first settled as a city by a party that included Negroes. Only recently has this fact been noted in the accounts students read in Los Angeles schools.

This overlay of recorded white achievement, buttressed by daily experience of white power—power to hire and fire, power to imprison, power to take Negro women at will—produced deep feelings of helplessness and self-doubt in many Negroes. This has been amplified in recent years rather than decreased because the mass media surrounded people on every hand with larger-than-life-size images of success and achievement. These images in magazines, movies, advertisements, and television were until very recently entirely in white terms. Even now they are predominantly so. It is no wonder that many Negro men deep down doubted their own capacity or their own dignity.

Nothing in their own folk culture seemed to be of any worth, except perhaps jazz and spirituals; and, in a way, this heritage taken up into the white culture seemed only to emphasize their role as jesters and clowns. White historic cultural values—as, for example, stubborn perseverance, success in conquering great odds, all the stout Puritan virtues—were by definition outside the Negro world.

Thus, the Negro has been deprived of a historical record which would give him a sense of fulfilling a destiny, of continuing an enterprise. And in addition he is surrounded by idealized history of white achievement which does not square with his experience with white people. What is most amazing in these days of breaking out of long-forged bonds, is that the bitterness and the hostility are not even greater. Education has in an ironic way become a part of the corridor toward full freedom for the Negro race in this country. It has not resulted in the grateful acquiescence to established white mores, that many expected. What is happening in the new generation of Negroes is the use of the analytic tools of the intellect, sociology, psychology, historical research, to discover the integrity in their own black heritage. This is consonant with what is happening in Africa and in other parts of the world. It brings a fresh new resource into American life—a people critical of the established assumption of our society, and yet fully an indigenous part of the society. It portends an infusion of dynamic new vitality that the country really needs.

Effects on the Negro of Current Daily Frustrations

In addition to the burdens of *history,* there are the continuing *frustrating experiences of daily life.* Despite the great publicity of gains in civil rights, due both to the new Civil Rights Law and to voluntary changes in the society, a great majority of Negro Americans are still feeling the daily pinch of discrimination. There are, in addition, tactless and often openly hostile expressions of prejudice. These cannot be dealt with in any case except indirectly. People are not preached out of their prejudice. They are forced out of it by events and experience.

But disregarding these social slights which are sometimes experienced by whites on other grounds, there remain certain structured barriers to full opportunity.

Despite fair employment statutes in some parts of the country, there are still many jobs and categories of jobs where Negro employees are not welcome.

There are still thousands of communities where Negro residents cannot buy homes if they have the money and the desire.

There are still thousands of schools where there is no, or at least only token, Negro attendance, even though there are many Negro families in the vicinity. And in those areas where law has supposedly dealt a death blow to discrimination, it is reluctantly complied with, in many instances.

This chapter is being written in a motel in a southern city, five months after the passage of the Civil

Rights Act. This motel, along with other facilities in the city, agreed to comply with the public accommodations section of the Bill. At least they said they did when inquiries were made in a Yankee accent.

However, when another guest with a more congenial accent inquired what they are now doing about Negro applicants who want to register, an elaborate scheme was described. The Negro is told that there are no openings or, if he has a reservation, that a mistake has been made. Generally, this is effective in discouraging further inquiry. Occasionally, however, a persistent person sits and waits for an opening. If a white man comes in, he is made out to have an advance reservation whether he has or not. If the situation is transparently impossible to lie about, then the waiting guest is finally given a room.

And so it goes with many areas of our common life. Despite the achievements of the past few years, despite the new sensitivity to discrimination of all kinds, the black man regularly faces the kind of blank wall and embarrassment that existed before. There may be hope for some; but, for a great many, life seems about as usual, with "the man" on top and you, either on the bottom, or wondering exactly what your position is.

For some Negroes who have been in the heat of the struggle there is the mounting frustration of seeing glimpses of full freedom, and then being reminded by history and daily experience that it has not yet materialized. Some turn under the intolerable burden of that disappointment, with real disgust, and repudiate the white man whose world they have wanted to inhabit.

And in the main, the white man goes his own road, disturbed by the crisis in color only when it seems to threaten him. Even the white liberal can escape the dilemma whenever he wishes. As someone expressed it, "The difference between the Negro and the white liberal who fight side by side for justice is, that when the day's battle is done, the white liberal can retire from the problem to his home, and the Negro takes the problem home with him."

The problem, however, is not his color. Increasingly, it is apparent that the militant Negro sees deep flaws in the social system itself which need attention, and he knows that integration into the existing society is not the final solution.

The new society, to be faithful to the American dream, must be more than the status quo white view of the good life. The Negro must bring into its making, the wisdom, the viewpoint that he has painfully acquired through living in but not really of the American democracy. There is real cause for concern whether this possibility will be realized without more dramatic hostility, more anguish.

There used to be a rhetorical appeal to become color blind, as the solution to racial conflict. What is now called for is to become more realistically and honestly attentive to the history and the sociology that make Negro and white citizens different and yet indissolubly joined in a common heritage.

4. The White Anglo-Saxon Conspiracy

From the early days of the nineteenth century there have been occasional movements of extreme nativism cropping up from time to time in this country. Nearly always it has taken the turn of defending the "original" pure Anglo-Saxon stock against the encroachments of newer immigrations—the Irish, the Italians, and in some quarters in later years, the Jews.

In the early 1830's de Tocqueville recorded his observations of the Anglo-Saxon American's fierce love of country which was then taking the form of extreme suspicion of outsiders and of pride in roughness in defense of the native land.

Dangers of Superpatriotism

We have had resurgent waves of this extremely emotional superpatriotism in this century. Right after World War I, the Ku Klux Klan had a period of activity in the South and in the Midwest. For the first time the Negro became a kind of threat to the insecure poor white. Linking together all the fearful unknowns in his sparse knowledge, although not necessarily in his experience, the fearful white became enamored of a giant conspiracy of Jews, Negroes, and Communists designed to overthrow the country. This died out in any significant movement in a relatively short time.

Again in the early 1950's, Senator McCarthy triggered this irrational streak of fear of subversion in his wild charges of Communist infiltration of the government.

The truth is that there had been a period in the late thirties and early forties when some people were attracted to communism, out of the disillusioning experiences of the depression. There were never very many, few ever got into any major position of leadership; and this period was well over when McCarthy began his tirades.

Again there was a lull, although there continued to be a larger body of people who considered themselves "conservatives" and who violently opposed almost all the changes occurring in the country which seemed to involve more federal authority, or changes in social customs. "Communism" became a loose charge directed against all those who held more liberal political opinions. This general antipathy was easily extended to include all who seemed not to conform to a white Anglo-Saxon image of the pure American. This was true even though some of the new Conservatives did not really belong to that strain. Nonetheless they identified with it.

The civil rights movement of the late fifties and early sixties aroused a great many more people who were fearful of Negroes, and then there began a new flowering of the nativist movements, with a great variety of shapes and forms.

The Ku Klux Klan was revived in the South, and a number of other organizations were formed of similar persuasion. The White Citizens Councils came into prominence in many southern communities in opposition to the new activity of civil rights groups. These were generally composed of local prominent citizens who were organized to resist, with a solid front, any breakdown in the policies of exclusion of Negroes in community life. They usually operated under the euphemism of "protecting the southern way of life." Frequently they were directly linked to the mayors and sheriffs of communities. In many places they were the voice of the total power structure of a town although, in many communities, established leadership resisted their influence.

In very few cases did these councils resort to the violence and terrorism of the Klan, except in so far as it could be arranged by the police in the line of duty, or instigated in jails among prisoners. These councils in many instances considered themselves as alternatives to the Klan, or the Klans, because there are many branches and split-offs of the regular organization. Individual members of these councils did, however, engage in harassment and petty violence.

A Closed Society

On the extreme right of the Klan, there grew up a terrorist organization known as the Society for the Preservation of the White Race. There appears to be some overlap between this body and the Klan membership. This society has endeavored to develop a new set of rationalizations for the same old diatribes. Byron de la Beckwith, who was charged with the murder of Medgar Evers, was one of the leaders of this organization in Mississippi. Its relatively small membership has been identified with a number of bombings and murders in various parts of the South, but it is difficult to trace these relationships.

In recent months the FBI has begun to take an intensive interest in these groups. After the murders of Michael Schwerner, James Chaney, and Andrew Goodman in Philadelphia, Mississippi, and the subsequent visit of Allen Dulles to Mississippi at the request of the President, the FBI moved in with force and vigilance.

Mississippi in 1963 and 1964 was the crucible in which the most determined civil rights forces mixed with the white terrorist groups.

Professor James Silver of the University of Mississippi has aptly described this state as a *Closed Society,* in a book by the same name. Here, ever since the Civil War, there has been a determined and well-nigh universal effort to keep the Negro as close to slavery as possible. This has meant a close working agreement among all the influential institutions of Mississippi society, the schools, the local and state governments, the newspapers, and often the churches. No crack was allowed in the solid front which held that the Negro was biologically and morally inferior, and that he had to be kept in his place. The usual southern social desires were rigidly maintained, separate eating facilities, separate public toilets, never referring to Negroes except by their first names—and also a benevolent support and affection for all Negro employees in the white family. These two attitudes went hand in hand —rigorous maintenance of caste and kindly supported charity.

This system was maintained in Mississippi long after it began to crack in other parts of the South. And it began to get ugly when it could not be maintained with grace and general consensus. As the old plantation system became automated in the Delta area of the northwest part of the state, the many thousands of illiterate field hands were not needed and were thrown out of work. The poorest state in the Union could not and would not care for their welfare or do anything to retrain them into useful jobs. Under Governor Ross Barnett, the state began a definite policy of trying to force Negroes out of the state to ease the economic pressure. These people, the least prepared for urban living, constituted an ever-increasing part of the migration into northern cities, particularly Chicago and Cleveland.

Barnett mobilized the entire resources of the state behind a last-ditch segregationist stand. A State Sovereignty Commission was established—which financed

White Citizens Councils out of tax money. The newspapers became even more shrill about the civil rights threats to the Mississippi way of life. The Governor defied the federal government over the admission of a Negro student to the University of Mississippi at Oxford. In the summer and fall of 1963 the White Citizens Councils became even bolder and began a systematic review of white churches to see that no integrationist doctrine was preached nor integration of congregations allowed to occur. By this time most of the liberal pulpit voices had already been forced out of the state, and now the councils were out to get even those ministers who chose to remain silent rather than preach the fundamentalist pseudobiblical justification of segregation that underlay so much of the emotional feeling on the subject. As Roy Moore, the head of the FBI in Mississippi, said, soon after he opened the expanded Jackson office, "These people think this is a religious crusade."

In the fall of 1963 students from Tougaloo College in Jackson, Mississippi, began testing the segregation policies of certain local churches, by going in interracial groups to morning worship. Though they were occasionally received and seated in some churches, in most instances, they were turned away, and sometimes arrested, in the charge of interfering with "public worship." Out of these arrests grew the case, *Poole vs. Barnett*, which attempted to reverse the issue and claim that the state was interfering with the church to deny people freedom of worship. In nearly all these church-going cases, the churches themselves did not prefer charges. Rather, members of the White Citizens Councils would station themselves outside the churches and direct the police in their arresting activities.

Such was the cohesion between government, power structure, mob, and newspapers in 1963. It was a frightening picture of native fascism. Civil rights workers not only could not rely on normal police protection: they feared the police. Beatings were frequent. All attempts to conduct voter registration or teach basic citizenship met with equal insults and intimidation.

Governor Paul Johnson, elected in November on an extremely racist platform, took office in early January and, to the surprise of many, announced a change in policy in state affairs. Though remaining a segregationist and denouncing all outside civil rights activities, he nonetheless has been very sensitive to the state's increasing notoriety.

On the day after his inauguration, an extensive voter registration drive began in Hattiesburg. For the first time this was allowed to proceed under police protection. The change in attitude had been communicated. He set out to make the state police a fairer and more professional law enforcement agency.

Nightriders and Terrorism

Despite the slight change for the better at the top, and despite other signs that the massive resistance was cracking, rural Mississippi still seethed with fear and hostility. Nightriders became even bolder in stopping people. On one such occasion, the chaplain of Tougaloo, the Rev. Ed King, a white man who has been prominently identified with civil rights causes, was stopped en route from Canton to Jackson. His carload included his wife, some Tougaloo faculty people, and a visiting professor from India. For over an hour, they were held prisoners in their car, while the Protectors of the White Race debated whether to kill them or not. Only the presence of the foreign guest finally deterred the nightriders. When the prisoners were released, they drove the thirty miles into Jackson, still followed by their attackers. They drove directly to the Governor's mansion, where they were shunted aside, as they were also when the incident was reported to the police.

Terrorism took its most frenzied toll in the planned murders of the three civil rights workers in Philadelphia, Mississippi, and in seventeen bombings in McComb.

These events are cause for real fright on the part of every American, and even more so when it is seen how these events were viewed by a majority of the good people of Mississippi. Though they were certainly not condoning the murders, they generally expressed feelings that these activities had been provoked by the presence of civil rights leaders in the states, by the "invasion" of student summer volunteers.

What the Federal Government Can and Cannot Do

The relation of the federal government to this pattern of organized intimidation and persecution in the name of a religious crusade has been upsetting. Civil rights leaders have viewed with increasing bitterness the helplessness of the federal government to protect people from this conspiracy while they are engaged in perfectly legitimate, Constitutionally guaranteed activities. The government, on the other hand, represented mainly by the Justice Department, has pointed out that there is no such thing as a federal police force nor should there be. Under Robert Kennedy, Nicholas Katzenbach, Burke Marshall, and John Doar, the Department has used every rule under its jurisdiction to see that abuses of Constitutional rights are brought to trial. There is a particularly trying conflict, because those in the Justice Department are deeply committed to the civil rights cause. They are also deeply hated by white leaders in Mississippi for their zeal. Nonetheless they do not believe that federal troops, their only final instrumentality, would help the situation except temporarily. They have been successful in 1964 in pressing the governor to be more effective in enforcing law and order with justice. In the meantime, those who suffer threat and intimidation with the full knowledge and sometimes participation of local and county police grow more cynical about their national government.

Who has really threatened the balance between the states and federal government? Is it Washington? Or is it Mississippi and other states, which refuse to take local action to protect people and to enforce the law equally for all citizens?

States' rights carry with them full responsibility for maintaining federal rights, else the Union is a mockery. The rights reserved to the states do not include capricious action based on customs which violate the full citizenship of anyone, resident in that state or otherwise.

It is a grave mistake to believe that Mississippi white conspiracy is purely local business, and unrelated to other parts of the nation. Its paranoid network of government and mob rule presumes to represent the opinion of thousands of people in that state. It surely does not represent all, because there are countless white people there who are ashamed of its reactionary stance. But there are great numbers who have been carefully taught over the years that they are a last-ditch remnant defending true Americanism.

A poll taken by Louis Harris in late 1964 characterized the extreme divergence of Mississippi opinion:

While the rest of the country was electing President Lyndon Johnson by a landslide this month, Mississippi was giving its votes to Senator Barry Goldwater by a staggering 87-13 per cent.

The profile of Mississippi public opinion behind this unique performance at the polls makes an illuminating case history of how local emotions can submerge the strongest sweep of national election trends.

Never before in election history have the voters of

one state so thoroughly dissented from the rest of the voters. Even in the other states which Senator Goldwater carried, except in Alabama where he was not on the ballot, Mr. Johnson got more than 40 per cent of the vote.

The President carried the South as a whole by 52-48 per cent of the two-party vote. The discrepancy is easier to understand when the attitudes of white voters in Mississippi are compared with those prevailing throughout the rest of the country.

Mississippi voters, unlike the nation as a whole, are dominated by the race question to the exclusion of almost any other political consideration. And whereas the issue of peace and nuclear control was perhaps the most powerful element in the minds of most American voters this fall, in Mississippi there are distinct signs of a trend toward isolationism and withdrawal by the United States from world affairs.

An analysis of the state of mind of Mississippi, drawn from an in-depth survey of a cross-section of that state's voters, also reveals that people elsewhere in the South are much closer on the national norm than their Mississippi neighbors:

• Against a pattern in the nation and in the South of general approval of Lyndon B. Johnson's performance in the White House, four out of five Mississippi voters are sharply critical of the job the President has been doing. (In central Mississippi Goldwater polled higher than 95 per cent in many precincts.)

• This criticism centers on Mr. Johnson's handling of race and civil rights problems (over 90 per cent unfavorable), but it spills over into such areas as foreign affairs, spending and keeping Communists out of government.

• While voters in the country as a whole look on themselves as "middle-of-the-roaders" (44 per cent), and the proportion holds for most of the South (43 per cent) Mississippi voters classify themselves overwhelmingly (68 per cent) as "conservatives."

• Nearly twice as many voters in Mississippi as elsewhere regard Mr. Johnson as either "liberal" or "radical." The Mississippi figure (78 per cent) is substantially higher than for the South generally (46 per cent). . . .

One of the keys to this disagreement over foreign policy is rooted in the apparent fears about Communist infiltration of government, which are by and large absent from people outside the state.

In answering a question about what major problems the nation faces today, Mississippians mentioned communism at home three times more frequently than Southerners in general and six times more frequently than Americans in general.

Even on civil rights, some sharp differences exist: while a plurality of people in the South still oppose the civil rights act, the division is close (54-56) per cent against; but in Mississippi, people oppose the legislation by an overwhelming 96-4 per cent margin. Furthermore, the South is almost evenly divided on the wisdom of sending in troops to enforce federal court orders to desegregate schools (52-48) per cent against, but Mississippi is opposed to such action by 93-7 per cent.*

* Quoted from an article by Louis Harris, "In Mississippi, Folks Do Think Differently," in *The Arkansas Gazette,* Nov. 24, 1964.

The Problem of the Radical Right

This extreme localization of the conspiracy is buttressed by a nation-wide resurgence in activities of the radical right. The nomination of Senator Goldwater by the Republican party made respectable for the first time in our history reactionary points of view in the nation by his being the standard bearer of a major party. His resounding defeat was reassuring in a way, but it was very encouraging to the extreme right, who were able to take a measure of their strength, really for the first time. Senator Goldwater himself does not seem to share the extreme views of racial hatred and prejudice, but he definitely was the candidate of these groups. The campaign weapons were based on the spreading of fear and unrest about the loyalty of all those engaged in leading our country. *None Dare Call It Treason* was the major printed piece used in the Goldwater campaign. This is a concoction of distortions and lies attacking the very foundation of our government. It does this in the name of extreme loyalty and patriotism, but it is designed to sow suspicion and distrust of everyone except white Anglo-Saxon people who swear allegiance to a highly mythological version of our past.

Among the major organizations and persons who lead this movement are several who direct their energies almost exclusively toward reactionary segments of American Protestantism. They are Rev. Billy James Hargis and his Christian Crusade, Rev. Carl McIntire and his American and International Council of

Churches, and Major Edgar Bundy and his Church League of America.

The fact that these three men are ordained ministers and claim to speak in the best interests of all true Christians unquestionably enhances their impact. They skillfully play on the fears of churchmen about the encroachments of communism in the church and American public life. They consistently and usually indiscriminately support radical right activity. They speak in the name of fundamentalist Christianity and are most persuasive with fundamentalist sects. But one should be careful not to conclude from this observation that conservative Christians are by definition adherents of the radical right. One unfortunate by-product of these men's insistence on speaking as fundamentalist Christians is that many fundamentalists who share few of their views and abhor all their tactics are nonetheless associated with them in the popular mind because of their shared theological conservatism.

Billy James Hargis, ordained in the Disciples of Christ, and Carl McIntire, ordained a Presbyterian, have both been officially purged from the ministerial rolls of their denominations, and their points of view thoroughly repudiated. Edgar Bundy, though he was ordained a Southern Baptist, has never held a pastorate and uses his Army reserve rank as a title.

Their favorite targets are strikingly similar: the Communist menace, integration, the National Council of Churches, the United States Government, the United Nations, the Supreme Court, the Roman Catholic Church, the Jews, and minority groups generally. All these they attack in the name of Christian faith and patriotism.

Although their methods vary, there is considerable similarity in the tactics they use. Their artistry lies in peddling half-truths as whole, and in seeing life in conspiratorial terms. For instance, after President Kennedy's assassination, Hargis maintained that this was a Communist plot, describing it in vivid detail, and that the subsequent murder of Lee Harvey Oswald was instigated by the Mafia. No one in his audience challenged him to substantiate his charges. And that's the pity, for unless such allegations are met with firm demands for documentation, they are all too often accepted as truth by ignorant and fear-ridden people.

From the headquarters of these three men, in books, tracts, and radio broadcasts, has flowed an ever-increasing stream of propaganda expressing their views. In 1964 the radical right spent at least $3,000,-000 on such materials. In 1965 they expect to double that figure.

One cannot dismiss lightly the persuasiveness of such men. Recently Arthur Larson, a Republican who is the former head of the U. S. Information Agency, said, in reference to the extreme right, "The mere saturation of this material is harmful. It is beginning to get into the bloodstream of people. Pretty soon ordinary intelligent citizens begin to believe there may be something to it."

Churchmen need to understand clearly and conclusively that the resurgence of the radical right in this country is only beginning. When it goes unchallenged, it flourishes. Whenever it is challenged with less than an all-out effort to expose it, it goes underground, only to reappear in new slogans and other subtle intrusions into the fears of people. This is the real "enemy within."

5. The Failure of the Churches

The outstanding fact about the churches is that with some major exceptions they have aided and abetted the Anglo-Saxon white conspiracy over the years.

A Possible Indictment of the Church

If an indictment of the church were to be prepared, it might very well read like this:

It is charged that the Christian church, although deeply involved in every part of the American nation, in its early days, and in the present time, has not influenced its adherents to practice racial justice in housing, education, job opportunity, and often public accommodations.

It is further charged that the Christian church in its own internal life has practiced discrimination, building barriers to prevent open membership in the very household of faith.

Beyond that, though preaching equality of all men before God, it has held its accomplishment really to be a long-time program, to be achieved gradually over the years.

This will seem an exaggeration to many, and they may begin a recitation of the forthright stands against racialism which various churches have taken over these same years. There are the shining exceptions. The major period of significant action was undoubtedly the abolitionist period in this country, and the years immediately following the Civil War. Strong-minded individuals like the Beechers and the Stowes blasted the ancient evil of slavery, and slowly church bodies began to take stands against the evil. Several of the larger church bodies divided over this issue, notably the Methodists, the Presbyterians, and the Baptists.

And there have been many and increasingly specific pronouncements against racial discrimination and its ills over the years. But, all in all, noting the exceptions with gratitude, the churches in this country have been dominated by society's equivocation and sometimes outright evil in the matter of discrimination.

One other qualifying explanation ought to be entered before moving to lay open this failure for scrutiny. The notion that slavery is a bad thing is a fairly recent idea in human history. Biblical writers knew slavery and accepted it as a normal situation.

The note of freedom for *all* is not particularly an old emphasis in Western civilization, and the Christian faith has had an important role in molding that culture. All too frequently the Christian emphasis on humility, self-abnegation, has been used as a prescription for others as well as a personal confession. Thus, Paul's admonition to slaves and masters to treat one another with respect due the relationship—"slaves obey . . . masters be kind . . ." became the authoritative Christian word on freedom in the society. For centuries the struggles to achieve democratic political rights for the common citizen tacitly excluded certain groups of people. "Blacks," "natives," nonwhites in any category somehow were related either to primitivism—more nearly animal than human—or to slavery, which carried its own rationale of legitimacy. These assumptions were as much a part of the life of the church as of the society. The Christian virtues of compassion and justice were thought of in terms that accepted these distinctions.

Thus, history neither justifies nor totally condemns the church. Human sin is pervasive of all life, in thought and deed. Men in possession of special privilege are not likely to be vigorous in stripping it away from themselves, particularly if there seems to be a long-standing precedent for maintaining it. Nevertheless, the fact of theological failure cannot be evaded.

There can be no other explanation for the white church's hesitancy, verbosity and ultimately little effort beyond tokenism in regard to its Negro brethren.

The most damning critique of our failure resides in the very existence of separate Negro denominations in this country. That it was not the gospel which was at fault is apparent in the decision of various Baptist, Methodist, and Christian groups to form their own fellowships. The Negro heard and responded to the glorious good news of Christ, but quickly experienced the fact that the new life in Christ, to be lived out in the church, could not be done in white churches. White church members often interpret the existence of the Negro church as being prima-facie evidence that Negroes really "prefer" to be with their own kind. This softened interpretation of the situation that produced the Negro church is a part of the blindness of the white majority. They do not comprehend the depth of the rejection that made it necessary for Negroes to organize their own churches if they were to worship in freedom and joy—two fundamental prerequisites of Christian worship. Indeed, perhaps they took most of both commodities with them when they left. Is this one reason why white establishment church worship is often so cold and sterile—the erecting of the forgotten wall within which white worship takes place?

It is not defects in the gospel that have created a church divided by color. Can anyone imagine the Head of the church, the friend of Samaritans, the destroyer of class distinction of all kinds, accepting separate cubicles based on affirmations of white superiority as being what the living Body of Christ should be?

It is only by mutilating Christ that men can justify theories of racial superiority. On World Wide Communion Sunday, 1963, several Negroes and whites were arrested for trying to go to church in a single body in Jackson, Mississippi. One church bulletin board announced the sermon topic for that day as "Keeping Christ in His Place."

What was intended was undoubtedly an exaltation of the Kingly Christ, but the events of the day preached the real sermon, and betrayed the real theology dominant there—a Christ limited to personal morality and emotional satisfaction—not the Christ of human relationship and interchange.

There are those who would be content to stop with the explanation that the church has simply failed to obey her Master. She has been sinful and disobedient to God by breaking the second commandment: "Thou shalt love thy neighbor as thyself." It is a self-evident fact.

But even Christ realized that men do not always understand plain language. Human sin veils an understanding. So Christ seeks to interpret the theological question, "Who Is My Neighbor," by a much more involved and yet more revealing explanation in the parable of the Good Samaritan. Neighbors, according to that beautifully sensitive account, are men whose lives touch one another, no matter how accidentally or distantly, and who come to one another's aid.

Thus, we have not said anything very helpful by declaring that the church has failed in the racial crisis in this country because Christians have been sinful and disobedient to Christ.

This is a good place to begin a confession. Indeed there is no other, but we must understand why it was apparently so easy for so many to be sinful and disobedient. There was a failure of theological teaching and understanding. I do not mean by this that any specific heresy has been widely taught and that that is why the church so long failed to see how compromised she was on the race issue.

Rather, it is a failure of propositional theology as a whole that makes the practice of heretical racism possible while preaching something different.

By propositional theology I mean the belief that doctrine is first to be clearly understood and then it can be applied. This is the commonest understanding of what theology is—the clearest and most logical interpretation of the central experience of the Christian revelation. Good theologians never have pretended that theology is the whole of the Christian enterprise. The experience of the living Christ, the life of prayer and praise, the ethical life are all part of the disciplines of the faith. Perhaps this is too modest a delineation of the task of theology and in this specific problem, namely racism, as in others, it leads to disastrous divisions between theology and practice. By propositional theology I mean the understanding that the teachings of the Christian church are logical and ideal distillations of the meaning of Christ for human life. They are then to be preached and taught to people who apply them to life. Thus, to begin with, there is acknowledged a gap between ideal teaching and practice.

In the main, propositional theology has made a clean case about racism. It is sinful, abhorrent to God, as indicated clearly in the interrelationship between the first and the second commandment taught by Christ.

Violation of the Oneness of the Human Family

In recent years, nearly every major church body has made clear pronouncements on the subject of racism and discrimination. It is categorically rejected. This understanding that theology is to be applied carries with it a hidden but powerful presupposition that you are free not to apply it.

This is at least one of the dynamic sources of the individualist emphasis so dominant in Protestantism. The belief that the gospel is heard as some pure, unattainable ideal, which individuals are then to take, figure out, and act upon, each separate from one another, is close to being the Protestant heresy. It is an anarchistic, self-worshiping doctrine, exalting each man's pride as the center of decision making. This exaggerated individualism (which finds its perfect exposition in Ayn Rand's theories) is enhanced by the idea that theology is something to be learned and then applied.

Even the character of the good attempts to become truly integrated in the church is tainted by this static conception of theology.

We have had decades of educational materials on the subject of race relations in the church. There have been study books, social action guides, exhortative material of all kinds. I would not want to dismiss these educational efforts as being useless. They have provided a reservoir of informed people all over the country. But most frequently it seemed that people read the material, nodded silently, or commented to their study group that it certainly was terrible, and "when was the world going to change." Even the most practical of action guides seemed pathetically inadequate. When integration is seen to be an aspect of a long-range goal of brotherhood to be achieved, then token evidences of this are given great importance.

How many churches salve their conscience with the single Negro member who belongs or, as is often the case, the instance of the Oriental family in the membership, trotted out on display as evidence that "we are making progress"?

Or, the doctrine of oneness of the whole human family under God (which is the second commandment) became twisted. The brotherhood of man is seen as an ideal, based operationally upon each man treating every other human being as if he were as *good* as he is. Personal goodness is a very precarious axis on which to hang the second commandment. To begin with, few of us deep down are very convinced that we are good, but often the image of our goodness is our most cherished possession. We polish it, we give people tantalizing glimpses of its radiance—if we are subtle, not too ostentatiously, only enough to impress people with our humility. Since our own goodness is not very real to us, relationships extended across racial lines—on the basis of others being just as "good" as we are—tend to be superficial and even condescending. Thus, much of the deliberate breaking of racial barriers has been suffused with patronizing. The black man as our "little brother," just as "good" as we are, is a very insubstantial base on which to build a true doctrine of the oneness of all mankind.

Whites have exacted from blacks the condition that they be loved for doing and being what we are to one another without any obligation at all.

Now, Negroes are beginning to exact from white people continuous demonstration that this old unconscious relationship is broken and thrown away. Alas, too much of it still remains within all of us, for it to be much reassurance to anyone.

Taking the Bible Literally

One of the aberrations of propositional theology has been biblical literalism. This is perhaps the worst form of the chaining of Christ in which the church has engaged. It begins with a very important concept: namely, that the Scriptures are the most continuously reliable source of knowing Christ and Christian teaching. But when you affix to this a wooden insistence that the poetry, parables, history, aphorisms, teaching, hymnody, dramas of the Bible, all be read as if the Bible were a scientific catalogue, then you are in bad trouble.

What you get is the exact opposite of accurate and deep understanding of Christian faith. You can read any previous emotional commitment into bits and pieces of the Scripture. Thus, the curse of Ham is extended (by what authority, no one seems to explain) to apply to all people of dark skin. Thus, the explanation that God has "set the bounds of the habitation of men" (simply a statement to explain the appearance of different nations in different parts of the world) becomes a defense of segregation. A much more apt conclusion to be drawn from this literal rendering of Scripture, would be a condemnation of white slave traders who seized black men from the bounds of their habitation in Africa.

The horror of the proof-texting segregationists is that they can escape the powerful punch of the parable of the Good Samaritan, while righteously distorting a verse to condone social sin. Governor Ross Barnett was for many years the teacher of a large Sunday school class in Jackson, Mississippi, propounding this kind of propositional theology in defense of the closed society.

Such abuse of Scripture is of course a decided exception to the main stream of theological thought, but among the laity it is shocking how influential literalism and individualism really are in buttressing prejudice. The appeal to the individual's right to sell to whomever he pleased was often given a religious gloss in the debate over the Constitutional amendment in California which outlawed fair-housing legislation. To turn the gospel around and make special privilege a "religious right" while ignoring the need for justice for one's neighbor is close to heresy.

The major deleterious results of propositional theology in this area, however, are a sense of impotence on the part of the churches, and a growing loss of respect for the validity of the Christian faith in the contemporary world.

A Fresh Look at the Christian Gospel

Now what is the opposite of propositional theology? It would be easy to counter with another adjective— "existential theology." This would be dishonest, although it would be less harmful than what we have, if properly understood. As a matter of fact, it is impossible to get away completely from proposition in theology—namely, the drawing of inferences, the building of meaningful systems of ideas.

What is needed perhaps is the beginning of a new set of propositions based on a fresh look at the essentials of the Christian gospel in the midst of these times. It is a sensing of priorities—based on a conviction that the Living God is at work in these moments of history, and that theology is wrought by an encounter between what we know of Christ in our historical religion and what we see in our contemporary life for him to touch and change.

We need to begin, in the field of reconstruction of theology in the area of racial tension with a fresh understanding of the *radical* sense of *human sin* the gospel reveals and the *radical freedom* the gospel offers men.

The Christian gospel, and indeed the Jewish understanding of life, is permeated with a profound realism about human frailty. The Old Testament is not a pantheon of idealized patriarchs and prophets. All the great figures of the Jewish heritage are men with clay feet. They rise to heights of prophetic courage, but they fail as well. All are flawed by sin and weakness. The grandeur of the Judaic faith is in this self-critical sense of being creatures and not creators. The New Testament, particularly in the teachings of Christ, is relentless in exposing the deceptions by which men seek to build their own virtue. The sinful thought is condemned with the evil deed.

The common thread of humanity, then, does not consist of goodness, or perfectibility—when men strive and rise above selfishness that is a cause for surprise and gratitude. The surer thing about us all, is our creatureliness—our begottenness, our fallenness. Thus, all men, to begin with, are as "bad" as I am. That is, we begin our understanding of other people from the position of our self-awareness as striving, egoistic, sensitive creatures—and all men are to be understood best from the depth of our own weakness. Thus, campaigns to win acceptance for Negroes by "whitening" them—always to a shade "whiter" than any living white man—die notoriously unsuccessful. The exaltation of certain Negro talents, musical and sports abilities particularly, is an aspect of the attempt to idealize; and so it dehumanizes every Negro who is not a Marian Anderson or a Jackie Robinson.

On a trip to Europe with a close friend who is Negro, we were seated at a table adjoining that of a classic type of southern white gentleman. He was mystified, and somewhat embarrassed, by these two friends, white and black, traveling together. Quite on his own he decided that the Negro passenger must be an entertainer and the white, the manager. Even after he found out that both were ordained ministers of the United Church of Christ, his mind would not let him accept this situation. To the end of the trip, he maintained the fiction firmly in his own mind, in order to make it possible for him to be civil to us.

The facts of the human condition are the place to begin theologically in the matter of relationships between the races. The history of slavery, the psychological bondage of the Negro even after the emancipation, unconscious self-deceptions practiced by whites, these constitute the stuff of the radical sinfulness in which we now live.

There are other aspects of this human condition which must not be glossed over.

One is the pervasive way in which powerful institutions in this country are related to the Anglo-Saxon white caste system. In recent years, southern Europeans, Jews, and some Orientals have managed to penetrate this upper-caste level of our institutional life; but they have done it by conforming insofar as possible to the white Anglo-Saxon Protestant image and mold, which the black man has not been allowed to do. His color and his slave heritage in this country have been impenetrable barriers. He is too visible a threat to the old Brahmin stock—or the image of that stock which persists even when the top dogs are named Romano or Hayakawa. The close identification of the church with this upper-middle-class image is a part of the burden the whole country struggles with as it seeks to become truly free.

Radical Freedom

The gospel is also about radical freedom. This freedom is not a laissez-faire individualism, license to act as aggressively in one's self-interest as one can get away with. That is radical bondage to tyranny.

Radical freedom is bondage to Christ in the most profound understanding of the faith. It asserts that even though all men and their institutions are heir to selfishness, they are also capable of miraculous self-transcendence. This self-transcendence, however, does not come about through bootstrap endeavor or Peale-istic self-exhortation. It is possible only in the abandonment of the "I" for the sake of the "we."

When this one concern is seen to involve the lowliest person, the most sinned-against brother, there you have the beginning of a freedom revolution that really is something. This does not mean that men or movements ever act purely—that is, without their own pride and pettiness being involved. This is not to be expected. Christ, however, is the sign to Christians that they should expect to live out their discipleship in some kind of pilgrimage on behalf of their brethren.

"Greater love has no man than this, that a man lay down his life for his friends."

The radical freedom of the gospel is precisely of this nature—that for the price of your life you win an unbelievable opportunity to help build a new community of human relationships.

This is where we have failed so miserably in our propositional theology—explaining what ought to happen to individuals and society if they truly followed Christ. Few people get preached into action. It was not until the shadow of turmoil actually touched some white people in the early 1960's, only when they began to break out of the frozen mold of "the way to behave"—in demonstrations and political actions—and were jailed, that the theology became clear. There must be a deed before there can be a doctrine that makes any sense. Commitment is not a decision to do something about belief, it is the belief that comes from having acted obediently to Christ, with self-concern pushed to one side.

There are those who fear change so much that they prefer death to freedom. The irony is that these are often the ones who are most preoccupied with abstract freedoms—a belief in it as an entity, or a view of it as personal privilege. Freedom is meaningful only *if* it is expressed in response to a higher loyalty; only when it is service, is it worth anything.

Because of a sterile view of theology the church has failed all too frequently in making any difference about its racial practices. She will be a witness for what is essential in the years ahead, only if her faith is radically joined to a realism about human nature, and an expectation that she can do "all things" with Christ —even help to bring about a fundamental reshaping of American society.

6. The Opportunity of the Churches

The year 1963 is the year America got a brief reprieve from a seemingly inevitable racial collision of major proportions. A culmination of ever-increasing pressures somehow focused for many people in the Birmingham demonstrations. Events moved many people, white and black, to a fear for what might happen if drastic new steps were not taken to alter the drift of the white society's basic indifference to the problem. A wholly new configuration of determination and action came into being, mostly out of desperation. Civil rights groups began to establish loose working agreements. And the churches began to take aggressive steps to work toward quick and basic changes. The "freedom movement" became a self-conscious enterprise. There were, of course, people working at it, long before 1963. The real pioneers, even of the immediate past, began sit-ins and freedom rides and the rest without any of the support of a widespread movement. Nonetheless, this sense that something new, of major proportion, was under way became a national concern in 1963 after Birmingham.

84

Sometimes people are shocked when you say that there are worse things that can happen to a city than a race riot. Generally, it is only after a dramatic flaring into the open of terribly suppressed frustration that people who are not living in a Negro ghetto begin to see the necessity for decisive action. A city that goes along with the lid on, making token gestures toward interracial good will and deluding itself into thinking that it can't happen here, is worse off than a city that has had the conflict, terrible as it is, made fully visible. The higher the complacency quotient, the more serious the problem is. So the tense times of 1963 were a great blessing to the nation—and to the churches.

A New Stance of the Religious Community

With the establishment of the National Council of Churches Commission on Religion and Race, and the strong comparable agencies in the member communions, we had symbolized a new stance on the part of the religious community. There had been voluntary bands of Christians committed to direct action before. The Catholic Interracial Council and the Episcopal Society for Cultural and Racial Unity were pioneers in this field. And there were official church agencies engaged in education about race relations (sometimes supporting direct action projects covertly), but for the first time the official instrumentalities of the churches commissioned direct action agencies.

These agencies, largely co-ordinated and spearheaded by the National Council's Commission on Religion and Race, found a place in the civil rights struggle with amazing rapidity. It was amazing because the churches did not have a very good reputation among other parts of the freedom movement. The exemplary work of individual clergymen in the freedom rides and other similar activities probably paved the way through the initial suspicion and distrust. It does not mean that militant Negro groups even now expect very much of the churches' efforts. They look continually for the time when the churches will get off the freedom train because the price has become too high. Movement people continually ask the churchmen anxiously about how the constituency is taking it. They fully expect that the white superiority people will finally call the tune if the church becomes too militantly involved in social change.

Certain events in 1963, 1964, and 1965, however, brought the church into a solid place in the freedom movement. These were (1) the establishment of active interreligious conferences on religion and race in many major cities; (2) the co-sponsorship of the March on Washington by the National Council Commission; (3) the persistent job of supporting the Civil Rights Bill for nearly twelve months in all parts of the country; (4) the volunteer service rendered in Mississippi by thousands of churchmen and the training of student volunteers by the Commission on Religion and Race; (5) the co-ordination of work in northern cities by religious forces, when the civil rights movement seemed hopelessly polarized; (6) the rallying of people to support the demonstration in Selma, Alabama; (7) the support of the 1965 voting bill.

The reprieve from disaster not only to the nation, but to the churches—for they bear a heavy burden of guilt because of their lofty idealistic stands on race— has given us time to do penance.

The real question before the churches is whether they are going on to the really substantive work that must be done. Participation in marches and campaigns for legislation is heady stuff. It brings some immediate gratifications. The question now is whether the same momentum can be maintained to help in the accomplishment of some permanent changes in our social order to insure the black man an unassailable place of equality.

Dangers of a Loss of Momentum

The danger of losing the *élan* of the freedom movement as we move toward community reorganization, political action, and other steps faces the civil rights groups as well. But the church is particularly vulnerable to the possibility that the high level of commitment will now be dissipated.

This is due to a number of reasons. First, a great many churchmen are basically uncomfortable about direct action in social change anyway. They feel that it makes for division within the church and beyond, that there is really danger in compromising the gospel by being involved in partisan issues.

The level of consensus was high enough in 1963-

1965 to permit unprecedented action. As the issues become focused on local northern problems, inevitably many churchmen will feel the squeeze themselves. Their ministers will become uneasy about action that embarrasses their laymen's business or political interests. Though the southern situation has many different aspects, because of its history, the reaction of the white laity to the churches' role in social change (as in Mississippi and Alabama) will prove not to be so different after all, when northern cities really become targets for civil rights action.

The churches are also very susceptible to faddism as far as special projects are concerned. Too often church leaders think in terms of "interesting programs" to keep the attention of the constituency. There will be many who feel that people are growing tired of "race" and that now we must move on to something else. "Poverty" is the study topic that has been moved to the forefront. Sometimes it is not apparent to people that these two issues—social justice and the abolition of poverty are integrally related—and that transcending both problems is that of giving powerless people in this highly technical and rich society an opportunity to participate in the society. It does not matter under what rubric, or indeed which program agency of the church, continuance in the movement is made possible. What is essential is that we not throw away the entry we have made into effective action, and that we not now retreat to a study-social-problems-in-limbo kind of orientation.

What can be done to prevent the loss of momentum, and in what directions should the churches be moving?

The best insurance against losing the clear focus many churches now have on the problem is the continued exposure of protected church people to their brethren who live outside the wall of white middle-class security.

This can be done partly by books. The confessional sort of polemic written by James Baldwin, LeRoi Jones, and, on the white side, by Bill Stringfellow may have been worth all the clear dispassionate analyses of the race problem ever written. There will continue to be this autobiographical accounting of what it feels like to dwell outside the gates of prosperous free America, while all the time you're being told you really belong to it.

Beyond the reading, however, there must be the continual intermingling of people from the two worlds —not only divided black and white, but divided "safe" and "precarious." The volunteer participation of students and adults in Mississippi and Alabama has done more to educate the churches in others parts of the country than nearly anything else. The kind of participation started in the ghettos of northern cities must be stepped up. There is a long tradition of church volunteers in social work ministries in urban areas. This form of volunteer work must now be expanded to include direct participation in political activity on specific issues affecting minorities and in the newer programs of training which will be made possible by the antipoverty funds.

In order to move into the next phase of the freedom revolution, however, it will be necessary for the churches to do far more than simply keeping their congregations up to date on what is going on. Only if the churches find some ways to participate directly in the next stages, so that they can help to bring about changes in housing patterns, job opportunity, school balancing and upgrading, will they fulfill the promises made by participation in these early stages of the revolution.

The over-all need in northern cities is for a co-ordination of effort on the part of all the agencies and groups working on intergroup relations, and choosing some targets for action. There are many suspicions between civil rights groups, and between such groups and the more indirect-action official agencies dealing with human relations. It will never be possible to achieve harmony of opinion along a continuum stretching from CORE to the Mayor's Human Relations Council. There should be communication, however, and agreement that there are different roles necessary in the long-term struggle. The more direct action groups, probably, are the ones of greatest consequence. They provide the impetus and the direction to which supporting groups can respond.

There is general agreement that demonstrations as such have limited usefulness. Now there must be broader strategies to effect political and social changes.

Each northern urban area must develop its own blueprint, but there are some common ingredients.

The primary goal is to give a more direct franchise to the increasing Negro populations, and help them prepare to exercise this franchise effectively. This means a whole range of things: voter registration drives, citizenship education (which includes a catalogue of subtopics such as how to organize political clubs, how the government works, who are the key people in positions of influence in the city, what the key issues are), political action centering on issues, implementing of the antipoverty program so that it really benefits those most in need.

There are so many jobs to be done and so many avenues of approach, that the great danger is that there will develop a whole bevy of competing interests. Also there is the possibility that unscrupulous political opportunists will move in and use these needs for their own advantage. Having abused and discriminated against Negro populations for a long time, certain political machines may now want to further exploit these masses by seeming to speak for them.

And in indignation against this exploitation *far left* political forces may once again find a fertile feeding ground. There is the possibility of an embittered radical left developing which will not be strong enough to effect any major changes, but will feed off a ruthless and politically corrupt political majority by attacking it, but never doing anything constructive about it.

That is one of the reasons why the churches must not now "cop" out of the struggle. Despite our reputation for timidity and captivity to the dominant power structure, we are the only institution that seems to have much capacity to transcend its self-interest, if for only brief periods of time.

The churches have the opportunity now of helping to organize these next stages of desperately needed social change in northern urban areas. They must participate in the establishment of working coalitions to change the centers of power, so that creative solutions can be brought to *de facto* school segregation, urban blight, cultural impoverishment, and the rest. They must support these efforts with money, with personnel, and—perhaps just as important—with their blessing. This authenticating role is of great significance. Most white people are terribly timid about social change. They are easily convinced that all change is a plot to undermine their security. The charges of "Communist," "Red," will fill the air when people in the ghetto organize to protest, or to register their opinions politically. The churches must interpret the meaning of events in a city in their moral and theological dimension.

Need for White-Community Involvement

However, it is not enough to give blessings and make endorsements. People from the churches must be deeply enough involved so that their endorsement comes from firsthand experience. This also puts them in the position of giving counsel and of legitimately fighting corruption from the inside of a movement.

This kind of coalition target-setting movement

ought to focus on the most visible key centers of change—perhaps a school board election, or a mayoralty campaign. Issues are paramount, but generally they are embodied in incumbents and candidates. People are what other people understand, far more easily than abstractions. The center of change for an urban area must be in the central city, in the midst of the people whose lives are most miserable. They have the most at stake, and all action must stay close to them. However, it will not be successful without the participation of intelligent and concerned people who live in the suburbs, both black and white. Allies are essential to bring about social change without producing deep chasms of bitterness that will produce long-lasting problems.

The white community must be involved. It must understand that the health of the whole city is endangered by building and containing ghettos of deprived people at the center of the metropolis. There will be thousands of whites who will never see this because they will be so threatened. But there are other thousands who do recognize the necessity of obliterating these great pockets of discrimination. These people must be enlisted in the struggle—by getting them to volunteer in specific campaigns of work in the inner city, by their becoming interpreters to their own neighbors in the suburbs both informally and through programs of adult education, and, most of all, by working actively to open closed residential communities to people of all races.

How can the churches organize themselves to participate in this phase of the movement?

It is unrealistic to think that congregations are going to move en masse to such involvement. Most congregations are more accurately "selective parishes," inclusive of people of all kinds of political, social, and religious opinion. They are not "gathered" into a congregation on any basis that will make possible consensus on the most crucial issues of the times. There are, of course, exceptions to this, and it is hoped there is enough consensus to make possible the grudging support of delegated bodies.

There is need for denominational judicatories and interchurch councils to authorize the establishment of agencies who are empowered to enter the struggle along with other public interest bodies on behalf of the churches. There ought to be built-in safeguards of periodic review; but, in the main, para-church bodies established by the larger structures of the church itself must be established.

Where congregations can come to consensus over specific projects and programs to implement social change, we should rejoice. However, the greatest concentration on the congregational level (particularly in the suburbs) ought to be in the matter of open housing. If congregations would really take the lead in this vital area, the problem could virtually be licked in five years' time.

The establishment of ecumenical church programs —Commissions on Human Rights would be a good name—properly supported by key clergymen and laymen would provide a fresh way of mobilizing the support of the churches. Perhaps the arena of action needs to be spelled out somewhat more carefully.

Arena of Action in Northern Urban Areas

The area is, first of all, the really hard core neighborhoods, which have been worked over by all kinds of social agencies with one interest or another. What is emerging in many cities is the need for genuine political action programs linked to services that will provide people with the necessities of life. This cannot be done through governmental agencies directly. However, various governmental programs can be used in a total strategy of work. It is essentially, however, a job of organizing the powerless. In the cities where there was rioting in the summer of 1964, most of the trouble was caused by young unemployed Negro youths who had nothing to look forward to and no real hope of things getting better. They did not belong to the civil rights groups, or to any other organizations. The alternatives clearly facing major cities are encouraging indigenous channels of legitimate political action (which might even at some times include peaceful demonstration), or wave after wave of rebellious rioting.

Strengthening the police is not the primary way to prevent rioting. It is only a necessary last resort. Indeed, the whole issue of the police has to be thoroughly examined. Often these officers represent to a frustrated and caged minority, the only visible symbol of the invisible white empire which contains them. They may be bad in their method and brutal, as they are in some cities, or they may be using up-to-date sociologically oriented methods. They still have two strikes against them because of what they represent. Therefore, they must use the most judicious and efficient of law enforcement procedures, devoid of harassment and sadism. They are very highly visible.

There are plenty of efforts now underway to make a concerted attack on apathy and frustration in the ghetto. Many church bodies own buildings and even have social centers in the inner city. They have pioneered in work there in the past two decades. Such centers as the Urban Training Center in Chicago are blazing trails to prepare people for work in the urban complex.

Other parts of the target are equally important, however. They include the marginal neighborhoods where fear of the expanding ghetto is greatest (some of these are the old-line suburbs), and the far-out suburbs where the population is overwhelmingly white. Someone has described the circle of white suburbs that surround the city of Cleveland as the chain of pearls that is choking the city.

In the marginal neighborhoods, perhaps the greatest need is to establish opportunities for interpretation of the needs of the ghetto, and also to build some alliances if possible. Often the schools are inadequate in these marginal neighborhoods as well as in the hard core slums. If a campaign to elect a more representative school board is launched, then the interests of the marginal neighborhoods should be solicited. Quality education, using bold new methods is what is basically at stake, and must be the context within which desegregation of school facilities takes place.

In the nearby suburbs, action and education programs must be linked to the problems in the center of the city. The Freedom Schools idea, so successful in Mississippi and during the northern school boycotts, might be adopted for use here. These centers of adult and youth education would use the same kind of curriculum: stress on Negro history, practical political education, and broader cultural interpretation of the issues at stake (Charles Silberman's *Crisis in Black and White* * would be good source material for this phase).

These Freedom Schools could be linked in a city-wide association with similar centers in the city proper and in the suburbs. They would also participate in joint action programs with other centers, and thus there would be the kind of shoulder-to-shoulder work that alone produces community. There are an increasing number of people in the suburbs who recognize the necessity of changing the situation toward a mutual sharing of the responsibility for the metropolis and its needs.

Insofar as possible these suburban Freedom Schools should be interracial in character. This is not so difficult as it seems, for increasingly there are Negro residential areas in the suburbs, carefully pocketed among

* New York: Random House, 1964.

the all-white areas. Here is a way to obliterate these real-estate Berlin walls. Churches ought to be the main possibilities as physical settings for such Freedom Schools, or whatever they might be called.

The Opportunity of the Southern Churches

I have been writing as if the main center of opportunity for the churches rested in northern urban areas. The next major thrusts must come in the North, in the movement as a whole. Therefore, the churches have an obligation to be useful servants of the oppressed here.

Their greatest opportunity—if access to centers of power and influence in the culture are used as measures—still remains in the South. This is the region where the churches still play a large part in the lives of people, where pietist and fundamentalist religion is still strong.

By and large the churches of the southern region have not played an active role in the civil rights struggle. A significant number of Negro churches have braved the hostility and been hosts to movement rallies and operations. In 1964, thirty-eight Negro churches were destroyed by fire in Mississippi. Only eleven of these churches, however, had even the faintest connection with civil rights activities. One suspects that the terror visited on these churches was directed as a warning to all Negro churches and to northern churchmen and the National Council Commission on Religion and Race for their active role in the South.

Southern white churches have abstained from direct participation. Many white clergymen have played important roles in the struggle for justice, if openly, often at the cost of their pulpits and, if secretly, then with terrible anguish and inner disquiet.

Frequently southern churchmen have said that this abstinence from direct involvement will make it possible for them to be agents of reconciliation after the worst of the bitterness is over. The time to enter this phase may be at hand. The much-attacked entrance of churchmen from other parts of the country and from national bodies may have succeeded in acting as a lightning rod for the hostility of the local white segregationists. This ought to place southern moderates in a free position to act now. The approach may be that at least they aren't so wild as those freedom riders or the National Council of Churches!

The time is very ripe for aggressive action to make possible the full implementation of the Civil Rights Bill of 1964. There has been a good start at compliance in most southern towns and cities. There are still many places, however, where there is little or no compliance, or only token compliance. There is a law now, and southern churchmen should move vigorously to see that it is obeyed.

For many years, it seemed as if the church in this country was becoming further and further isolated from the arena where decisions were made on public issues. A way has been opened, through the strong stand of some churchmen in the middle phases of the freedom struggle for this trend to be reversed. We were not very much involved in the decisive early stages (1954-1960), except for certain outstanding clergymen. We have begun to find a role that people count on in the years 1960-1965. Will we carry through, or will this moment pass into the ashes as a last spark flares for a moment before the log lies finally cold and still?

7. The Power of the Churches

For nearly twenty years the standard refrain of those concerned about Christian social ethics has been that the church was hopelessly captive to American culture. There has been plenty of evidence that this was so. A growing popular religion, elevating a blend of pietism, personal improvement, and patriotism seemed to be the dominant religious motif. The early fifties had what was popularly described as a religious revival, but most astute observers commented that it was really a renewal of church attendance and membership, a manifestation of a search for roots by those caught in the restless surge of a mobile society. People began moving in every direction—to the suburbs, up the ladder of income, back and forth across the nation under the personnel changes of great corporations. And the church became the one symbol of the old values. New church building, particularly in the newer suburbs, became a billion-dollar-a-year phenomenon in this country.

It was apparent that this new interest in the church, accompanied also by some renewal of interest in lay theological study, was symptomatic of deep hungers for personal security and transcendent meaning to life.

Over all hung the power of a burgeoning technological society, whose drives and needs seemed to call the tune, with the institutions of religion playing variations.

Background for the Freedom Movement

The thoughtful voices of the religious community almost uniformly warned against the superficiality of the religious revival and pleaded for heeding the prophetic message of the Judeo-Christian tradition. But the popular religious leaders were those who either symbolized the separation of the religious message from the problems of society—à la Billy Graham—or saw the faith as a sanctifier of American individualism, à la Norman Vincent Peale.

Within the Christian community, there was a remarkable unanimity of opinion among social ethicists. They recognized how interrelated the church was with the whole American scene. Despite the tradition of separation of church and state, the predominantly Protestant ethos had surrounded most of the public enterprises of America for nearly two centuries. The public schools, although officially nonreligious, were suffused with Protestant presuppositions—inculcated by generations of lady Protestant teachers and principals. In most parts of the country, the leaders of industry, banking, the professions, and political life had been the stalwart lay leaders of the Protestant churches as well.

As Catholic and Jewish leaders came into prominence, the role of Protestant church influence in the public domain seemed to recede. However, in most places, the Protestant upper-middle-class dominance in the field of economics, and indirectly behind the scenes in politics, was maintained. The more behind the scenes it was, the more indirectly the life of the churches seemed to be connected to public issues.

The white middle class, looking to its leaders, more and more took its opinions from secular and programatically expedient policies, derived from their new role in American life. It was generally acknowledged that the white Anglo-Saxon Protestant view of American life was to be maintained only by the broadest kind of American consensus—including white Catholics and Jews in a generalized world view. The church was to be kept for one's private life, a reminder whence we had come, a private shrine to rekindle the drives toward integrity and fair play. What happened to the Protestant white American became the model finally for Jew and white Catholic as well, and with nearly as much determination to keep church and synagogue private or ceremonial matters. One has to be sure to qualify this properly. Both Catholics and Jews retained enough of the memory of being minorities in this country to want to keep some corporate relationship between their religion and the public realm.

Protestants, in the main, were willing to abandon any connection between public policy and religion and doctrine, because they felt sure that the broad consensus of American opinion was and would remain broadly Protestant. This misidentification of the American dream with essential Christian doctrine is a part of the failure of propositional theology discussed in an earlier chapter.

A real rift developed between the opinions of the better-trained white clergymen and their laymen. The clergymen were appalled by the misunderstanding of propositional theology and the insistence that faith was only a personal matter. These clergymen, and some laymen, grew more and more pessimistic about the role of religion in American life—seeing it increasingly as an ornament, without substantive influence. Strong laymen, on the other hand, often reacted with increasing frustration to the clergymen. Either they deplored the concern of their ministers for public issues and turned to pseudoreligions (the John Birch Society and other far-right organizations are really heretical religious movements), or they despised the church as not being worth bothering about except for ceremonial occasions.

The Negro church had a quite different role. The Negro was so isolated from the centers of decision making in this society that he developed his own parallel world—often modeled on white society, but not in the matter of religion and the common life. White people have not always understood this (nor have some Negroes), for they have misunderstood the emotional, dramatic worship life of many Negro congregations as being a symptom of escape. A clearer interpretation would be that it was more nearly a celebration of the integrity of a point of view, in which the common life and the personal life were closely linked to the divine. It may have been a withdrawal from the impact of the rejecting white society, but it was affirmatively related to the Negro world. Negro ministers have generally remained involved in matters affecting the whole community. As the conflict developed between the Negro and the white community, as the Negro sought to establish his rights to his whole citizenship, Negro ministers and churches have played a decisive role.

It is in such a context that the freedom movement began to move and expand—white churches walled off by custom and consent from direct participation in public affairs which were controversial, and Negro churches deeply involved in all concerns of the community which affected their people. There were major exceptions to this observation in both black and white churches, but the generalization is valid.

The racial crisis began to threaten many of the shibboleths by which we had been living. Clearly Negroes weren't by and large "happy" with their isolation, and clearly a naïve trust in a long slow process of evolution (nurtured by education and building good attitudes) was not the answer.

As the pressure and action mounted within the Negro community, many white clergymen were shamed into direct action themselves. Finally, the churches began to take official action, and beyond that to move with enough of the consensus of membership so that an effect was felt.

Impact of the Church on the Civil Rights Bill

The concerted effort to pass the Civil Rights Bill was one of the most obvious exercises of a new mobilization of power. For the first time in history, a single Protestant-Orthodox, Roman Catholic, and Jewish testimony was presented to Congress in support of legislation. Congress became aware that the religious community was aroused in a startling way. The participation of the religious groups in the March on Washington was another bit of evidence. Over 40,000 white church people participated in that March. It is easy to look back at that event and recall what an inspirational spectacle of dignity and affirmation it was. It is easy to forget what terrible foreboding preceded the March, the dire predictions of violence and disaster in the nation's Capital. The churches were denounced for being naïvely a party to such a potentially dangerous event. The Southern Presbyterian representatives to the National Council of Churches declared their nonsupport of the National Council of Churches' involvement in it. Government people nervously wished the whole thing would evaporate. Newspapers almost uniformly expressed misgivings and hostility.

In retrospect, it becomes apparent that this event was the major turning point when "the Movement" became more than just a Negro concern, but a coalition freedom movement in which it was recognized by thousands of whites that their freedom was at stake too.

White church people followed through during the long months of 1963 and 1964 with unparalleled persistent attention to the legislative process. Thousands of calls were made on Congressmen and Senators.

I shall long remember one such visit to the Speaker of the House of Representatives. With us was an Episcopal bishop, looking every inch an Anglican divine, broad-brimmed hat and umbrella as a part of the equipment. At one point in the conversation, the Bishop pointed his umbrella at the Speaker and said, "I have been coming to Congress for many years, asking for one reform after another. It was presumed that I represented at least some church people. Now, Mr. Speaker, I *know* I speak for thousands."

The Congress felt the continuous impact of the church's influence for the passage of the strongest possible bill. At one point, Administration leaders felt their only chance of passage lay in a watered-down bill. Church pressure insisted on the stronger version which was finally passed.

Continuous meetings in Washington, and finally a two-month continuous assembly of church leaders made known the fact that there could be no result other than passage. In the Midwest, where irony had placed the real fate of the passage of the Bill in the hands of Congressmen whose districts did not include many Negroes, church influence kept the "moral question" clearly before the people, and thus before the Congressmen.

When it was finally passed, friend and foe alike credited the passage of the bill to the persistent power of the church. Senator Humphrey, the leader of the struggle in the Senate, and other veteran fighters for civil rights legislation, insisted that the churches' efforts had made the difference which had been lacking in other struggles for such bills. Senator Russell declared that it had passed because "those damn preachers had got the idea it was a moral issue." Various enemies of the bill had tried many ways to stop the church's participation, even setting the Internal Revenue Service onto the National Council of Churches for an investigation of violation of tax exemption. A careful investigation revealed that the Council had not violated the lobbying prohibitions.

Church Focus on the Mississippi Struggle

In the Mississippi struggle, the role of the churches through volunteers and aid to the civil rights organizations made a significant difference in focusing the concern of the nation there.

There was great reluctance to take off the lid of the closed society that was Mississippi, particularly in Washington. The situation was so oppressive, and federal jurisdiction short of troops so limited, that it seemed like a foolhardy thing to encourage any direct challenge of the white supremacy system. The Justice

Department had been through some bad times with Governor Wallace in Alabama and with Governor Barnett at Oxford, Mississippi. It was thoroughly sympathetic with the drive for civil rights but reluctant to encourage anything that might cause white Mississippi to react with hostility. The rest of the nation, the whites at least, simply did not believe it could be as bad as civil rights workers insisted it was.

Certain of the younger civil rights workers, those mainly in the Student Nonviolent Co-ordinating Committee, were committed to challenging the awful tyranny of Mississippi. The NAACP, on the other hand, experienced in the travail of Mississippi injustice, did not want an open confrontation.

The Commission on Religion and Race decided to support the more aggressive group, within the law, but with the firm conviction that the time for change had come. All the volunteers who went into that state knew full well the great personal danger they faced. Hundreds of ministers also went to Mississippi as chaplains. A full-time, long-range program of community redevelopment known as the Delta Ministry was begun by the National Council of Churches with the aid of the World Council of Churches.

The national church bodies, incurring the wrath of local church groups because of "outside intervention," helped to authenticate the rightness of the freedom revolution in Mississippi. It brought the attention of the federal government inevitably to bear on the situation. At times federal authorities relied heavily on the church bodies for impartial inside information as to what was going on and frequently responded to the urging of the church groups for more federal action there.

At the time of the Allen Dulles visit to Mississippi at the request of President Johnson, following the death of the three young martyrs of the civil rights struggle there, Mr. Dulles made several recommendations. One was the stepping-up of FBI activity in Mississippi (this was done and made an enormous difference in the state). Another was to urge the closest collaboration of the government with the National Council of Churches ministry in Mississippi.

The extraordinary response of churchmen from all over the country to the crisis in Selma, Alabama, in the spring of 1965 was a decisive event. What the nation had begun to suspect was now corroborated—the churches could make the difference.

In Selma, Roman Catholics for the first time entered direct action demonstrations in great numbers.

What have been the main sources of power that the church has tapped in these past programs, which have brought it into the main stream of public action in the racial crisis?

First of all, it has been due mostly to the fact which the prophetic voices of the church have been decrying all these years—namely, the deep immersion of the church in the culture. The very complicated way in which the church is involved in middle-class American life has given it power. The church has outlets in every part of the country. This was the envy of every other agency trying to work for the passage of the Civil Rights Bill. Protestant denominations and inter-denominational agencies are often ridiculed for their complicated bureaucracy. As the campaign to inform people about the moral issues involved in the legislation proceeded, it became apparent that this organization was very useful. Indeed, much of the church's organization is a proper response to a highly organized society. To be effective you must have it. What has been wrong with it, has been that it was so often preoccupied with self-culture, simply the perpetuation of itself. When it was turned outward to deal with an issue for the sake of the whole people, it performed effectively, and with a spirit of relief that at last there was something it could support with enthusiasm.

Power Derived from Unofficial Status

The church has power in the country because it is *unofficially established*. The doctrine of separation of church and state had prevented the abuses of special churchly privilege or dictation by the state, for the most part. But there has been the role of the sanctifier of values which people have given to the church. Oftentimes this role has been badly used, as a sanctifier of the most self-righteous and chauvinistic clichés. But like it or not, the honest fact is that this same relationship of the church with the middle-class, solid American virtue made a strong contribution to the civil rights struggle at this juncture. It broadened the consensus on the rightness of the struggle. It made possible the acceptance of social change by great numbers of people in the country, who would normally have rejected it as too radical.

Now this role of the church is viewed with suspicion by many of the more militant civil rights leaders. They feel that the church may only soften the sharp impact of the protest against injustice. Some worried about this during the March. They felt that the whole thing might turn into a tea party by the participation of the religious community. Given the history of the church in this country, these aggressive leaders are wise to look with some suspicion and mistrust. They can never take for granted that in the future the church will always take firm stands simply because justice and right demand it. The church is too much a folk institution for that. It must be viewed in the dimension of its response to constituency and all the other attributes of a large popular middle-class institution.

Indeed, the test is just ahead, as to whether, the way having been broken open, the churches can follow through with what must be done to help complete the revolution.

Will the churches give real support to growing Negro power in securing their rights in urban areas? Will they help to secure better schools? Will they aid in the process by which Negroes obtain power? Will they help to open up closed residential areas to Negroes? Will they use their considerable economic power to further equal opportunity in American industry? These are the crucial decisions now to be made. Will all these steps seem too threatening to white special privilege, and therefore to be ruled out of bounds as "political" or "extremist"?

The Church's Willingness to Take Risks

The second source of the church's power in the struggle has been the willingness of the established institutions to take *risks*. That is what convinced the Negro civil rights leaders that some trust was possible. It is what convinced legislators and other government officials that the church might be worth listening to at this juncture. If the leaders of the church, which is seen popularly to be so related to middle-of-the-road and even conservative opinion in this country, were willing to risk making mistakes that might lead to embarrassment, then the issue simply must be serious. That was what underlay so much of the possibility of action. The glimmer of evidence that the churches might be taking the gospel somewhat seriously—a gospel which involves a Cross, suffering for the sake of one's brother—this gave the church power. So many people have experienced the church only as exhorter to be and to do things which did not threaten the minister or the church as an institution. More and more laymen are aware of how desirous they have been of keeping the real power of the church under proper control—namely, the appeal of Christ to risk one's self for the sake of the brethren.

Many laymen are also becoming aware of how important it is for this American society to engage in some major cultural appraisal of itself—particularly at the points of poverty, employment in a rapidly automated age, and the superimposed pattern of social discrimination.

There are really three major options open: (1) the government must assume more and more responsibility for public problems; (2) a kind of antigovernment radical right fascism will be allowed to feed on deeply troubled Americans; or (3) private sectors of the society must take on responsibility as partners (and critics) of government to preserve freedom by extending its privileges to more people.

The threat of irresponsible reaction frightened many people during the 1964 Presidential election. It is hoped that many laymen now see that the churches can be a responsible agent in the public sphere, through which they can work at particular points of social crisis. This does not mean that the churches should try to take the place of other private agencies in the social field nor that they should participate in partisan political campaigns as a "Christian" party. The attention of the church agencies should be centered on issues, but occasionally this may mean supporting individuals who are identified with issues.

The far righters, from Welch to McIntire, who most castigate the churches for any role in the public sphere, are themselves heavily engaged toward one end, capturing the American mind for dangerous reactionary political opinions, with which racism is a steady companion.

The oversimplified answers of this Far Right group appeal to people who are frightened by the strange new age we are moving toward. They prate about "freedom" as if it were a commodity defined by individual white achievement. All efforts to extend freedom to others or to do social planning so that in an advancing technological age, the many will not be crushed by the few, are attacked as socialism or communism. Yet the very heart of democracy depends upon the balance of responsible government and vigorous nongovernmental institutions. Laymen who are uneasy about too much government, and who yet reject the mirages of the Far Right, may indeed participate in agencies of the church to work for the social changes necessary for full freedom for all Americans.

If the corporate support of the church is now withdrawn from the struggle, then there will be no channel of communication between the struggles in the ghetto and the white power structure. For this revolution to succeed, without major collisions, there must be some responsive points of empathy in the white middle class.

The churches must provide the instrumentalities to bridge the gap. The dangers of the church and state confusion of interest need not materialize. The church must not become the tool of political or governmental policy. And the church must not blackmail the state into special privilege or favors. The church, and allied religious agencies, can continue to be a third force between direct action agencies and official bodies working in the field of human rights. This requires a vigilance and a sophistication of personnel the churches have not always possessed.

Accompanying this use of power, based on responsibility and openness to risk, there must be developed a new and more mature view of churchmanship, on the part of the broader constituency. No one must feel that he is read out of the church if he does not support a particular action program, sponsored by a special agency of his church. On the other hand, unless power to make tactical decisions in the public realm is delegated to such an agency, the church will wither away into a chain of family shrines where ancestor worship becomes the only kind of activity allowed.

Power in a Common Faith

The third source of power that the church possesses in the freedom struggle is some of the relationships that exist between Negro and white churches. They claim the same Lord. They have had many experiences of working together. The white churches have also engaged in patronization of their Negro brethen. All has not been as it should. Nevertheless, there is more mutuality of concern and experience between the races within the church than in most other communities of interest. Therefore this common faith, and common experience, may provide one of the major channels of communication between the races, when others break down.

Bitterness is sure to increase as the pressures increase in northern cities. Perhaps the fellowship of the church, black and white, may be one of the few places where frank talk can occur without a complete breakdown of communication.

There is plenty of secular power available to the church to be a determining factor in the freedom revolution. This secular power is not antithetical to any "spiritual" power, inherent in the gospel. It indeed is at the center of the Incarnation faith. This must be fully understood, or there will be a strong withdrawal from effective action as being unfaithful to the central teachings of the church.

A wedge must not be driven between power and spirit. If that occurs, then the churches in this land will indeed have lost their greatest opportunities to be truly servants of mankind.

8. The Power Beyond the Churches

In the pages of the Bible there are many contradictions, many unexplainable bits of legend and history. There are discontinuities and puzzling lapses into primitive religion from high plateaus of ethical insight. And yet the God of the Bible, though veiled from sight and elusive of definition, is perfectly clear in his deeds. He is the All-Powerful One who has chosen, perhaps among other things, to concern himself with the affairs of one of his creatures, Man. So inexplicable is this interest, that the Jews could only assume that it rises out of sheer love. The Bible is an account of how this frightening, and yet alone satisfying, love shaped the history of a people. It is surely seen from man's side of the gulf fixed between God and creation. And yet the common events of that history are so God obsessed, that it is not necessary to keep saying, "So it seemed to them."

God, a God of Deliverance

The God of the Bible is a god of deliverance. He has made men in the image of divinity and yet they are incorrigibly tempted to make gods out of their own self-interest. He punishes them, woos them, teaches them through prophets and historians, goads them, haunts them with glimpses of what the uncorrupted human life would be like. And again and again he delivers them.

In Christ, the Bible is fearless to proclaim, God takes the boldest step yet. He becomes man, in order that men may see even more explicitly the destiny of the whole human race.

In Christ, the love affair between one people and God is extended to include the whole human race. Christ is the new Adam, according to the vision of Paul.

Now the modern man has three choices when he takes the Bible and tries to relate it to our times. He can reject the whole thing as outdated mythology of no significance, save for historical interest. He can take it pretty much as it is, and meticulously try to fit an ancient-world view with an utterly different twentieth-century view. Or he can accept on faith the basic truth of the Bible—that God is a living one, who is known to the extent he can be known in the struggles of men to live beyond themselves.

Such a view as this last, alone, makes any sense to me. The God men glimpsed in Jesus Christ is still the model on which much of the world builds its imagery. In a fantastically complicated civilization, men still struggle for justice, the right relationships between men; and they struggle also for love, that elusive mutual acceptance between men. It is these concerns that make history at all, struggles for love and justice against the perversions and failures forever corrupting these attempts. Modern man has the choice between viewing this struggle as an absurdity or as a part of a purposeful power.

Biblical faith views the passion of men for fulfillment as a part of God's plan. It does not see all human events as predetermined. All kinds of possibilities are open to men, individually and collectively. But it is God who haunts them when they are wandering, and it is God who delivers them when they have been set upon by insuperable odds.

There is no separate sacred history as far as biblical religion is concerned. The life-and-death matter of Joseph betrayed by his brothers, a people starving in the wilderness, a rabbi killed for his naïve goodness —these are secular events and God's events, all at the same time.

If one believes in such a God, then the events of the times in which we live have religious significance. It is not necessary to beatify the freedom movement in order for it to be seen as more likely delineating the power of God in these times than the meeting of solemn religious assemblies.

The whole human race is encamped once again by the Red Sea. Will it be engulfed by the terrible forces that the clever shamans have let loose—destructive hydrogen bombs, or mechanically clever devices to enslave the whole race to idleness? The human spirit is aching with anxiety about the future. And, in addition, some parts of the human family are still kept in slavery because of their color. I believe that the God of our Fathers will deliver us.

Men as Instruments of Deliverance

I believe further that this delivering God has raised up men as instruments of that deliverance to himself. He has never left himself without witnesses. It also seems clear that those faithful to the call of the Divine may not be in the churches, or perhaps not even willing to acknowledge that anyone is calling their names.

Because the power of God is always behind any movement that struggles for justice and compassion, it does not necessarily follow that automatically it will "succeed" in the sense conceived by its adherents, or that it will be protected from suffering.

That is the meaning of the Cross. What seems utterly to fail and to be destroyed may so fill a whole generation with power that the world is changed. That which seems glibly acceptable to a whole nation may be cast down in a day. All human events stand under the mysterious ordering of that which cannot be captured or tamed.

At the same time, some laws of history are also laws of life. They are aspects of the radical sense of human sin and of the radical freedom of which the Christian gospel is revelatory.

All movements to free people are likely to be opposed by those who profit by having a subjugated race. Conflict of some sort is inevitable, when social change is underway. Not to expect this, and not to be willing to face it, is to be foolishly naïve about human nature. What is more, it is often the "good people" who oppose change, because their self-estimate is related to the relative security they enjoy. The "good people" are also susceptible to as many desperate tactics in the struggle as the uncouth down-and-outs.

The "good" people often allow the "not quite so good" people to do the dirty fighting, while they remain aloof from the battle. This has been the pattern in Mississippi white society. Klansmen and rednecks have done the terrorizing and the murdering of Negroes and civil rights workers. The "good people" professed ignorance of the whole thing, but were extremely reluctant to bring to trial the "not quite so good" people.

All men are sinners. That is a fundamental fact to know not only about our enemies but also about ourselves and our allies. Because people are caught up in a struggle for human dignity, it does not follow that they are all without human vices. This is one of the great shocks that many idealistic people experience who find a new cause for living in the freedom movement. They discover that there is heavy competition between groups and leaders, that personal ethics may not always be on a high plane; and they are deflated. People are heir to the sins of the flesh and of the spirit, though their cause be just. In fact, living under heavy pressure and tension—possibly even danger to life— is not conducive to developing Elsie Dinsmore qualities. But the *cause* is not invalidated. The Movement needs stern critics from within. Such critique is not easy to give, because any embattled group is extremely sensitive to the possibility of betrayal. Also the cohesive spirit of a group depends to some extent on idealizing the group. A little of this is not serious, but heavy inhalation is deadly.

The Crucifixion reminds Christians that human sin is a deadly fact. It is the most consistently pervasive fact about men. The Crucifixion also stands as a sign that radical human freedom is possible. Whatever your theological view of Christ, the straight historical fact is that the murdering of a remarkable rabbi named Jesus of Nazareth, set loose in the world a powerful vision of human power—deeply ethical, passionately committed. Committed Christian or not, one must acknowledge that Calvary is a kind of axis of Western history.

The power of a good man willing to die for his brethren is an unquenchable power. When that kind of commitment is translated into a movement, it can make changes that every wise observer would say would be impossible.

The possibility of beneficial and permanent changes in race relations is a very real one. It takes commitment, though, and the willingness to try unpopular courses of action. You surely have to risk being called a Communist, although the irony of that label being applied loosely to all who are committed to the eradication of injustice is amazing. The only bulwark against communism, in a world looking for social changes among the masses, is a movement dedicated to change which takes into account the radical destiny of man—sinner and free man. This, communism does not do.

"Indeed, according to the Law, it might almost be said, everything is cleansed by blood and without the shedding of blood there is no forgiveness" (Hebrews 9:22, NEB).

In the summer of 1964, flying out of Jackson, Mississippi, on my way to New Orleans, I sat across the aisle from a nun. Having just come from a visit to the headquarters of the Mississippi Summer Project and to the National Council of Churches' ministry there, I pricked up my ears when I heard her discussing the students in Mississippi that summer with her seat companion.

She was decrying their presence in Mississippi on the grounds that their misplaced idealism would only provoke violence on the part of the local white supremacists. She said she wasn't questioning their dedication nor even the rightness of their position, but surely it was a bad thing to stir up people who felt differently and thereby create danger and turmoil. All the time she was speaking she was fingering a very large crucifix which hung around her neck.

The terrible irony of what she was saying, of course, escaped her—namely, that the one whose sign she held most precious would never have set his face to go to Jerusalem, would never have hung upon that cross if he had believed the thesis she was expounding.

This nun is symbolic of much of the church today. It knows what the gospel is, intellectually. The church today is better informed about nuances of theology, liturgy, and the rest than any other generation of Christians, but it finds it painful to acknowledge Christlike action in the world. This is supposed to be a secular age, which has rejected Christian dogma— indeed, dogma of all kinds. These unruly people who disturb the good people in the practice of their religion have to be faulted for their excesses.

The real questions that sensitive people need to ask in this time are "What is God doing?" and "How can I respond to his call?" The church also needs to ask these questions.

Providence has given the church a treasure house. In this country, the church can be found in every corner of the land. It is rich and powerful. There are those who would discount it on these grounds alone. What body voluntarily divests itself of safety? Perhaps only the church can, because the words of Christ are still heard and they still sting: "He who would be first shall be last," "Take up your cross and follow me." Other words which have been raised to the position of Holy Writ, "The church must not contaminate itself with politics," or "The church has a spiritual mission" (meaning in this case an abstract message), must be judged by the Scripture. There we behold God the mover of men, the deliverer of the oppressed.

The Fate of the Freedom Movement

It is quite possible that the freedom revolution will receive the fate of many movements in a mass society. It will be written about, and displayed so crassly, that it will disappear like fluff. It may be only a catch phrase.

But for a brief period of time, the deep, unflinching aspiration of the Negro American, and some of his white friends, found here an instrument of liberation from oppressive and insulting abuse.

Whether the "movement" survives or not, in its present form, there are people who will not stop struggling for a more equitable society until they die. It is not too early to say that something as significant as the Abolition Movement or the Labor Movement has been born.

What shape it will take is not now visible. It may flower into a new kind of peoples' radical movement—made up of the dispossessed, the don't-quite-make-its, and also the goal-less youth of our times. This in itself might not be destructive. We badly need challenges to the assumption that all is completely right in America.

The church may be able to help, at least part of it, by being called once again to the clear imperatives that Christ's life and death keep before it. The church could bring strength to the movement. It could bring channels of communication to more isolated parts of the society. More than that, it could bring a realistic critique based on a sane doctrine of man. It could bring color and drama, and the inner disciplines of the mind and spirit. It already has given first gifts in all these areas. What haunts us now is whether it can continue to deliver its share of resources. This may well be how its usefulness is measured a century hence.

It may even make the difference as to whether or not it is to exist a hundred years from now.

The test of the power of the church now is purely a pragmatic one—if its full panorama of resources is considered—money, people, theology, worship. The power of God is not under question.

He is bringing into being new shapes and centers of human community. We must praise him. We must, as Christians, acknowledge both the continuity and discontinuity with the past that we claim as our heritage.

In July, 1963, I was in Egypt. Actually I was in Savannah, Georgia, at the peak of the tension in that city. Along with leaders of the SCLC, we convinced the leading white clergymen of that city that the tension generated by the jailing of all the responsible Negro leadership in the protest movement, and the deadlock over further progress in desegregation in that city, meant that grave disorder and violence were a real danger.

In the evening, I went to the protest meeting held on the outskirts of the city. The scene that evening was one I shall never forget. As a white person coming to an illegally held meeting in the Negro ghetto, I was questioned closely and inspected thoroughly before I was allowed inside. Here was a group of about a hundred people—women with their dresses and persons burned by tear gas, young men bandaged and battered, and all in a near state of hysteria, as a result of the pressures they had been subjected to through the preceding days. They were singing the songs of freedom without pause, in a growing crescendo of desperation: "Before I'll be a slave, I'll be buried in my grave, and go home to my Lord and be free." "We shall overcome."

One often uses a phrase, "an atmosphere filled with tension." This is the first time in my life that I experienced this to be a physical fact and not just a figure of speech. One knew that the lighting of a match in the room would have produced an explosion.

Andrew Young asked me to speak to them about the concern that other Christians felt for them. Words come very cheaply when you are only a visitor in Hell. But I could speak of the Commission on Religion and Race and other acts of Christian witness and what they represented about the determination of American Christianity to end the evil of racial discrimination.

I had the strongest feeling that I was in Egypt on the night of Passover, just before the time of deliverance. The twelfth chapter of Exodus records, "It was a night of watching by the Lord, to bring them out of the land of Egypt; so this same night is a night of watching kept to the Lord by all the people of Israel through their generations."